Praise for Worth

D0242912

TAMILE TEMOONYAH, AUTHOR OF *THE*

SEVEN TYPES OF SPIRIT GUIDE

Worth

An Inspiring True Story of Abandonment,
Exile, Inner Strength and Belonging

Bharti Dhir

HAY HOUSE

Carlsbad, California • New York City
London • Sydney • New Delhi

Published in the United Kingdom by:
Hay House UK Ltd, The Sixth Floor, Watson House,
54 Baker Street, London W1U 7BU
Tel: +44 (0)20 3927 7290; Fax: +44 (0)20 3927 7291
www.hayhouse.co.uk

Published in the United States of America by:
Hay House Inc., PO Box 5100, Carlsbad, CA 92018-5100
Tel: (1) 760 431 7695 or (800) 654 5126
Fax: (1) 760 431 6948 or (800) 650 5115; www.hayhouse.com

Published in Australia by:
Hay House Australia Pty Ltd, 18/36 Ralph St, Alexandria NSW 2015
Tel: (61) 2 9669 4299; Fax: (61) 2 9669 4144; www.hayhouse.com.au

Published in India by:
Hay House Publishers India, Muskaan Complex,
Plot No.3, B-2, Vasant Kunj, New Delhi 110 070
Tel: (91) 11 4176 1620; Fax: (91) 11 4176 1630; www.hayhouse.co.in

A catalogue record for this book is available from the British Library.

Tradepaper ISBN: 978-1-78817-485-5
E-book ISBN: 978-1-78817-486-2
Audiobook ISBN: 978-1-78817-598-2

Printed and bound by CPI Group (UK) Ltd, Croydon, CR0 4YY

This book is dedicated to the memory of my dear father (Kartarchand Dhir) and my dear mother (Pritam Kaur).
I value their blessings as spiritual angels in my life and their assistance in writing this memoir.

Contents

Prologue

Uganda, East Africa – 1967

I t all began when we were driving out to the savannah one day on what turned out to be a magical occasion. Dad loved taking us out to see the wildlife and he used to show us the tracks made by zebras, leopards, lions, antelopes and other creatures. Suddenly, he stopped the car and signalled for us to be silent.

The next moment, a steady stream of elephants traipsed along in front of us – maybe a hundred, it seemed to me – kicking up dust clouds as the ground shook beneath them and the herd made its way into the bush. Only one last elephant remained, stopping right in front of us, in close proximity to the car bonnet. We gazed at this beautiful creature, hearts pounding in a mixture of both excitement and trepidation. My father felt we were too close, so he put the car in reverse, letting the car roll back silently before engaging the handbrake. We wondered what would happen next as we waited and waited.

'What are we waiting for?' my brother whispered. 'All the others have long since disappeared. Why isn't that one following?'

'Shh,' my father hissed. 'Watch and wait.'

There was no obvious reason why Dad didn't just drive round him. It wasn't as if the road wasn't wide enough, after all.

It must have been a good twenty minutes later when a mummy elephant appeared with a calf clutching her tail as they darted across the road in front of us. The elephant watching our car raised his trunk, trumpeted his thanks and calmly followed them.

To me, Dad was the cleverest man alive. He must have known the elephant was waiting for his family to join it. I was in awe. How did he know two more members of their large family had yet to follow?

Years later, I still think of that day. Dad, the elephant, the guardian of our family. Mum, the mother elephant. And me, the baby – lost, only to be rescued by a mother who would never have left me behind, let alone to my own fate.

~

Introduction

This book is for anyone who is ready to build their self-worth and sense of belonging. Through my life story, I hope to inspire you towards growing your worth. If my journey helps to restore even the smallest sense of belief that no matter what life throws at you, you're valuable and loved, it'll have been worthwhile.

During my life journey, my worth has been shaped by both negative and positive experiences, just like yours. The challenges:

- being abandoned by a roadside at birth

- dodging more bullets than I'd like to admit – and by this, I mean physical bullets, when escaping former President Idi Amin's Uganda

- being of dual heritage: Asian–African

- growing up among those with the inherent prejudicial, judgmental notion that I'd turn out to commit the same deed as my birth mother by having a child out of wedlock

- my illegitimate status, with so-called dirty blood bringing potential dishonour on the family

- born female when males were so revered

- being a refugee from Uganda

- settling in a strange country

- the misery of an incurable skin condition, epidermolysis bullosa, the belief being that this was fatal

- suffering from systemic lupus erythematosus, an autoimmune condition, the belief being that I wouldn't live long

- the loss of my adoptive parents

What I've gained from these experiences is the knowledge that we can *all* change our destinies and find our true purpose in life. The fact I'm still here despite the odds is testament to this fact.

My 'destiny' at birth was certain death at the hands of another. Just because there was a belief that I wouldn't survive, it didn't mean it had to be my reality. When the voices of doom said I was going to die and that it wouldn't be possible to go to university, hold down a career, become a mother, I still never gave up on my dreams and aspirations. My life didn't have to head in the direction they were suggesting. Destiny, the Divine, angelic forces, call it what you will; fortunately for me, the way my life was mapped out by others wasn't my reality. It wasn't meant to be. Whatever people said my destiny was, it didn't happen. So with this in mind, the knowledge that we can all change our destinies is so incredibly powerful. And you can hold on to that knowledge that you can change, too.

To heal me from my agonizing skin condition, epidermolysis bullosa, my parents sought the advice of gurus, who said I wouldn't live to be a teenager. Imagine their anguish and desperation on hearing this. A parent should never have to have to think of burying or cremating their child – it just isn't the natural order of things.

This book deals with the emotional erosion of self-worth that conditions like these can bring – and how I found my own way through it. I now live a full life with a daughter of my own and a career as a social worker helping children – but I spent many years in the margins not knowing who I was, or what my values were. Throughout this book, I use the word 'mum' when I'm referring to my adoptive mum and 'birth mother' to signify my biological mother.

I understand what it is to be displaced and I know first-hand the prejudice that often comes with it. I was rejected by some in the Indian community in which I grew up in Uganda because I'm illegitimate and dark-skinned. As a girl and then a woman, my Indian culture sought to control every interaction I had. I was set apart because of my illnesses, shunned and bullied at school. I had to learn how to discern true friendship from false, to gather strength on the inside rather than seek others' approval. These challenges have given me a strength that I share with you so you, too, can nurture your worth, which is your birthright. Not only that, but wrapped within my own story are also those of others whose courage, belief and strength are equally remarkable.

My journey to worth is very much a spiritual one – one that led me to walk away from traditional religions, instead bringing me a personal relationship with the Divine and my guardian angel. Angels have protected me every step of the way and whenever I've faltered on my path, I know they've helped my sense of worth to grow.

My aim is to show you that no matter who you are, what pain you're in or what you feel inside, you're a human being worthy of love.

~

CHAPTER I

Wild Imaginings

'No, please don't. I beg of you, please don't.' The young woman lifted herself off her bed, wincing in pain. She tried to wipe her tears in a futile attempt to see better. 'Please don't kill my baby – please, look... I've suckled her for two days. She's so innocent, so helpless. Can't you see – she needs me.' She clutched her elderly aunt's arm and tried to snatch the baby from her aunt's arms. 'Look, we'll go away... far away from here. No one needs to know I've had her. No one. I promise you – no disgrace will be brought to this family....'

A stinging slap across the cheek silenced her pleas.

'You've already disgraced us,' her aunt spat. Another slap followed. 'You've acted like the prostitute you are. Now, you shall bear the consequences of your shameful behaviour. Death is the only outcome for that bastard child of yours.'

The young woman caught the eye of the elderly servant, Edgar, who had witnessed the scene. Mutely, she pleaded with him, appealing for him to come to her aid. An unspoken message passed between them – the child wouldn't be harmed.

The aunt turned and looked coldly at her niece.

'Things didn't have to end this way. Blame this shameless hussy. My poor sister, God rest her soul…. She'd be turning in her grave with a daughter like this.'

Anger spilt over and the aunt landed blow after blow on her niece.

'Thank God my sister didn't live to witness this, you cursed witch,' she hissed. 'First, you killed her in childbirth. It should have been *you* who died! Then we wouldn't have had to see this day. I swear, if my sister were alive now, she'd surely have died from the shame you've brought upon us.

'I demand that you take her now and dispose of her in the river, Edgar. Get her out of my sight this instant. I can't face seeing her a moment longer.'

'Forgive me, madam,' Edgar said, intervening, 'but I must insist you have a little heart. She's suffered enough. And she'll suffer for the rest of her life, knowing her baby will surely die with what you're asking me to do. Let her at least hold the child one last time.'

The young woman rained kisses on her baby's face, rocking her, clasping her tightly. The aunt looked at her niece and a deep weariness took over.

Edgar bent to my birth mother. 'Pass me the baby, miss, for we must leave now. The longer this takes, the harder it'll be. It's best to give her to me now. Prolonging the inevitable won't help anyone.'

The young woman didn't plead, didn't cry, merely followed his softly spoken command.

'Her name is Fatima, Edgar – it's Fatima.' She spoke with conviction, looking at her aunt defiantly before averting her gaze.

Edgar walked away slowly, the young woman's baby in his arms.

'Edgar. Don't even think about defying me.'

The older woman blocked his path, searching his face for any clues that he might disobey her order. Then, with a sigh, she moved aside – the large sum of money he'd been given would ensure compliance.

Sending a silent prayer that the baby would remain asleep, Edgar stepped from the house and hailed a passing driver, who agreed to give him a lift. Edgar sank gratefully into the air-conditioned coolness of the car.

Well before they neared town, Edgar asked the driver to pull over, not wanting to encounter anyone who might remember him. The car disappeared into the distance, leaving the road in darkness, not another soul in sight.

Turning, Edgar noticed a box by the roadside, the promise of fruit luring him forwards, knowing how in Africa it's customary for weary, hungry drivers to stop and buy fruit and vegetables. Only, when he lifted the lid, he found it empty, giving him an idea. After gently lowering the sleeping baby inside, he closed the lid, said a silent prayer and walked away. Fatima's fate was now very much in God's hands. If He wanted her to live, she would. If not, then she'd die.

Figuring she was now God's responsibility and no longer his, Edgar continued his journey on foot towards town. His family would be surprised but delighted to see him.

In the box, the baby stirred.

———

'So there I was, on my way home from work, hungry and in need of sustenance. But why that particular box, I'll never know. I tell you – the Almighty works in mysterious ways. Mysterious ways, I tell you...'.

Mrs Owaza sighed wearily as she started clearing away the plates. She'd heard the story a million times since her husband had happened on that baby. Indeed, he'd even taken copies of the article in the newspaper that had been released with the headline 'Man Rescues Abandoned Baby Girl'.

There was a paragraph beneath a photo of a solemn-looking Mr Owaza with a baby in his arms. You couldn't exactly say her husband was gazing into the baby's eyes – judging by the pose, he seemed more interested in looking into the camera. Mrs Owaza snorted at his seeming disinterest in the baby in favour of his own appearance.

Mr Owaza frowned. *Why was it*, he thought despondently, *that when the whole world was holding him up as a hero, his own family had no such regard for him?* Even the children disappeared as soon as he started to tell the story of how God had meant him to feel hungry even though he'd eaten earlier. How he'd passed so many boxes that must have been overflowing with the most delicious fruits. How he'd been drawn to this one particular crate of fruit, curiosity having led him to lift the lid of this solitary box to see what was inside.

He'd found a sleeping child wrapped in a pink cotton sheet. Imagine! Mr Owaza then went on to tell the newspaper that he'd had an argument with the farmer who'd appeared out of nowhere to sell him his fruit.

The farmer had accused him – a respected, moral, upstanding member of society – of trying to foist his unwanted offspring on him. The farmer told him that his child would be better off staying with Mr Owaza, as he already had seven mouths to feed and he certainly wasn't going to bring up another one.

'Look at me,' Mr Owaza had cried indignantly. 'Does this look like my baby?' He placed his hand against the baby's face. 'Light,' he said, referring to the colour of the baby's skin. Then he waved his own hand. 'Dark!'

'All babies are light-skinned when they're born,' said the farmer, unperturbed. 'I'm just letting you know, sir, that I wasn't born yesterday. You people, with your fancy suits and fine cars – you're the worst, carrying on behind your wives' backs. Taking a lady friend, having an affair with this woman or that woman and then finding yourself in trouble. I've seen it all before.'

The farmer began to pack up his fruit, ignoring the offended Mr Owaza, who stamped his foot in rage.

'This is *not* my baby, you imbecile. I stopped for some fruit and merely looked in the box!'

The farmer started heading in the direction of the bush.

'It'll be dark soon. Just leave it there and the hyenas will get rid of it...'. He turned and looked slyly at Mr Owaza. 'If that baby isn't yours, sir, then walk away. It's neither your business, nor mine.'

Mr Owaza's disbelief and curses only made the farmer laugh more, after which he disappeared as swiftly as he'd materialized.

'What could I do?' Mr Owaza looked imploringly at his audience. 'I'm a man – a simple man. I'm also a Christian – a God-fearing one at that.'

Murmurs of approval were heard along with cries of 'Hear, hear...'.

'Well, God had led me there and so I had to fulfil my calling,' Mr Owaza continued. 'I picked up the box. That baby was wailing. The sound went through me. I tell you – it went through me. But I did my duty and I took her to the police station, where I told them what had happened. They took her to hospital.

'My God-given task was complete!' He looked upwards. 'I'll always be honoured that I was chosen. I'll always be honoured, I tell you... Have you seen my photo in the newspaper? Look at this one. I had it framed...'.

'Anybody for dessert?' Mrs Owaza said, laying bowls on the table as Mr Owaza's story ended abruptly, the guests turning away from her husband in anticipation of the delicious sweets on offer, his story forgotten.

There were times, though, when Mr Owaza pondered what had happened to the baby. He knew she'd been taken in by an Asian couple, though he wondered if he'd ever get to see her again and imagined another framed newspaper cutting years later: 'Hero Thanked by Girl he Rescued.'

So here I am, that little rescued girl. I've never met my rescuer, but I've entertained so many scenarios about how I came to be on that roadside. Many of us do – those of us foundlings who were discovered on hillsides, riverbanks, or on the doorsteps of hospitals, churches, temples. Those who were left behind, with no birth mother coming to claim them. That rejection, that knowing that I was left to die or be found, though, fired my imagination. Every scrap of gossip surrounding my discovery was retained in my memory. Together with the newspaper cutting and adoption paperwork carefully kept in a file by my adoptive father – which is all I have – it fuelled a new scenario. It's amazing what you conjure in your head with so little to go on. It's a way of making sense of all the disjointed information as you piece together the few facts and many fictions.

I've always loved books, stories and daydreaming. While I was chided by teachers and my parents for not paying attention because I was lost in a dreamworld, I believe that the daydreams and stories I interwove helped me to keep a sense of my self-worth. I'd laugh aloud at some of the stories I made up and that laughter helped to alleviate the feelings of rejection, confusion or pain. The stories helped me to protect my sense of worth, as they gave me permission to explore a situation that was impossible for a child's mind to process and fully understand.

In these stories in my head, my birth mother was always young and vulnerable. She had an affair with a man her parents disliked; she was from a rich family or a poor family. She always wanted to keep me, but society wouldn't let her.

When we started living in England, my mum, my siblings and I were always on the lookout for bargains because we were existing on income support at the time. On Saturday mornings we'd eat the last of the week's food – my favourite packet minestrone soup with bread and butter – and take a trip to the jumble sale at the local church, then in the afternoon we'd go food shopping. The jumble sales were outings we looked forward to, but we sensed how our poverty hurt our mum.

If we ever went to a high street clothes shop to look around, we knew we'd never be able to afford to buy anything. Whenever my siblings and I announced that one day we'd have the money to buy this or that, Mum would say, 'One day when you're all working, you'll be able to afford it.'

I'd dismissed that idea in a flash – there was no way I was going to wait around for years until I was old enough to work. I'd wanted us to be rescued now. And so, in my daydream, my birth mother would suddenly turn up and envelop me in her arms. Then she'd profess how sorry she was and that she'd never wanted to get rid of me. And about how she'd discovered I was now living in England and she'd come to get me. But then I'd insist she had to take my family with her, too, because they were my family, as well.

In my mind, my birth mum would agree. It turned out she was a queen and she'd sweep us all into her palace, meaning my adoptive mum would share in all the riches she'd strived so hard for. Well, at least that's the fairy-tale ending that a subconscious part of me never stopped yearning for. For no matter how loving your adoptive family is, the dream is forever with you – an archive of footage you've created with your imagination that can bear multiple replays and rewrites.

It was these daydreams that helped to build my sense of worth, making me believe that I'd get there one day. By get there, I mean that I wished for a time when I could have enough money to buy new clothes from a shop rather than a jumble sale. Get there meant never feeling short of money. I needed to have that hope, to know that I could reach a point where I could walk into a shop one day and buy something new, or at least have enough money not to have to struggle to buy food. My musings also protected me from feeling ashamed about my second-hand clothes, having quickly learned that if I said I got whatever I was wearing at a jumble sale, people would look at me with a mixture of shock or pity. I'd also learned to pretend that I hadn't noticed the looks exchanged and instead encouraged them to go to jumble sales to see what bargains they could pick up, too!

Of course, deep down, I knew there would be no magical rescue, but I allowed myself my daydreams because they lifted my soul. I didn't know it then, but now I see that those fantasies were actually wishes being manifested for my future life. Today, those desires for financial security, for having the means to buy new clothes and shoes, have definitely come true – and so much more besides.

Perhaps adopted children born after me dream less about their imagined birth families because they're now given that information in a Life Story – a book that contains photographs of their life prior to the adoption, along with details of their birth. A Later Life Letter written by the child's social worker is also given to the child's adoptive parents, which details the circumstances surrounding the adoption – in short, stating what led to the child being adopted.

The Later Life Letter is passed to children by adoptive parents when they're ready emotionally to have the questions about their past answered, should they choose to know the facts. This is invariably when they start asking questions about their past, which is how you recognize they may be more receptive to learning more about their background, otherwise known as their life experience. It's a full background history right up to the point of adoption, so the child is not left with unanswered questions. But for me, during the 1960s and 70s, all I had were my stories to make up a background – my imagination, which formed a cloak of protection around my fragile sense of identity.

Locals who reportedly knew my family used to say that my birth mother was a mystery woman who'd turned up on the outskirts of our small town of Kabale, in south-west Uganda, along with her aunt and brother. She'd told no one of her pregnancy, keeping it secret from everyone, her burka concealing the growing bump. So when they disappeared and I turned up a couple of days later, they all made the assumption that I could only have come from this family.

Back then, it was normal for the local Asian women who formed part of my mum's friendship group to get together at each other's houses for tea a few times a week. The mystery woman and her aunt attended these gatherings but rarely talked about themselves, and the woman they believed was my birth mother never spoke at all, keeping herself to herself. After several months, the aunt and the mystery woman, as well as her brother, suddenly disappeared. They didn't say they were leaving, never mind where they were going, and they never mentioned where they were from. It was all very strange.

I was told that I was found on the roadside a day or so after their departure, so the whole town started surmising that the young mystery woman must have been pregnant, given birth to me in secret and abandoned me before vanishing. It was said the woman was Muslim and some told me my real name was Fatima, not Bharti as I'm now known, meaning that I might be a Muslim by birth.

Apparently, a servant was asked to throw me in the nearest dam. He was given a huge amount of money to drown me, but he just couldn't bring himself to do that to a defenceless baby. In the end, he decided to place me in a box and leave me on the roadside, which is the story I've shared with you in this book.

According to other sources, my birth father was a servant at my birth mother's house and he'd got her pregnant. He was immediately sacked and the family subsequently moved. It was only when my discovery was reported in the newspaper that he realized that the abandoned baby was his. He told the judge that he wanted to keep me, but questions were raised as to why he'd not come forwards sooner, as I was seven months old by then. By then, my parents were about to adopt me, so he'd demanded hundreds of thousands of shillings in compensation – which the judge denied: if he'd wanted me and cared about me, he wouldn't have asked for money.

This resonates with a psychic reading I later had with a guru, who told me that my birth father's anger at not being able to claim me had led him to curse both my adoptive parents and myself, creating negative karma. The guru said that my birth father wished my adoptive mum and dad to suffer greatly for having kept me. And he'd cursed me by giving me this illness (epidermolysis bullosa), knowing that there can be no greater suffering for a parent than to see their child debilitated by constant pain and then to die. The guru explained that my birth father had also wanted my adoptive father to suffer financially (I guess that was because my birth father hadn't been paid anything when he'd asked the court for the money before granting or allowing the adoption). It therefore seemed that he'd achieved this, too, as my adoptive dad forked out a fortune in order to find a cure for me.

I don't know how these stories came about. Whenever I asked people how they knew these tales, no one would commit. They'd all be subject to rumour and gossip, the individuals concerned having just heard it somewhere or other. To my frustration, no further explanation was ever given.

I wove a tapestry of stories around my conception, birth and abandonment. I tried to fill the many gaps in my background with imagined scenarios because even to this day I don't have anything like a full account. I just have the police report and adoption papers, which my parents kept and which I came across when I was around seven years old in 1967, and then again this year, 2020. It states that on 5 September 1960, I was discovered alive in a box at only a couple of days old. Apparently, I was looked after at the hospital for two weeks or so, at which point hospital authorities advised that unless I received a mother's nurture, I probably wouldn't survive.

According to the report, attempts were made by police to trace the mother of the infant – me – but without success. It's thought that an Asian woman came from the Masaka area to Kabale specially to have the child and that on her return journey she abandoned it. Now, the police file has been closed, as the general consensus is that no good purpose can be served by continuing with enquiries.

Even after my adoptive father died, my adoptive mother still refused to tell me anything about my origins, often skirting the issue. I couldn't understand why I hadn't been told about my adoption and for some reason, as a teenager, I determined to have this discussion with her. I felt angry when random people said we weren't related. My adoptive parents always saw me as being part of their family completely, not believing or treating me any differently, so to them it wasn't an issue. Yet, it had led to all sorts of issues in school for me. It was something I needed to understand.

At the time, I related an experience I'd had as a young child to my mum, in which I remembered seeing a strange man standing outside our veranda, holding a machete. I'd seen him before and I recalled feeling a sense of shock at that revelation. I'd first seen him in the street, when my sister Anju and I had been walking to our first primary school. He was wearing faded khaki shorts and a khaki jacket – the type of outfit hunters wore. Only this man wasn't dressed like the foresters who carried machetes to cut down the bush. Or like the gardeners who carried their scythes from house to house – we didn't have lawnmowers then. This man had walked alongside us, not right next to us, and he'd stared straight at me.

While I felt curious at the time, I didn't think about him again until we came out of school later that day. But then he came back another day, once again watching me from a distance. Only that time he followed us until we were nearly home. I remember turning round and found myself giving him a smile. He bared his teeth at me in a snarl or grimace and disappeared. I had a very bad feeling and I knew I needed to stay away from him.

And then he'd reappeared on our veranda.

Mum looked visibly shocked when I told her, and while she encouraged me to speak all those years later, it seemed she almost didn't want to know more.

'I saw him coming through the gate onto the veranda while you and Dad were having a siesta. Two of the servants went up to him and I could hear them talking to him in low voices. It was like they were warning him off.

'One of the servants pointed at me and then the man took a step towards me. He still had the machete in his hand. The servants stood right in front of me, blocking his way so he couldn't get any closer.

'And then just as soon as he'd come, he went. Just vanished back into the street.'

'Why didn't you tell us at the time?' Mum was pale, all vestige of colour having drained from her face.

'Because I didn't think it was important, Mummyji.'

There were tears in her eyes. 'But that was very important. Something could have happened to you.'

'What could possibly have happened to me? Who was he, Mummyji?'

'You don't need to know.'

Mum's reaction made me feel she knew more than she was letting on, so I asked, 'Do you think he was my birth father?'

It was clear this wasn't just a strange man and that this was something significant. There was clearly a lot more to it, but then she wouldn't talk about it.

She turned away. 'Why bother with such questions? We're in England now and those days are behind us.'

I wanted to persist with my line of questioning, but she looked so shaken and distraught that I couldn't bear to put her through it and ask again. I had to surmise that the man was indeed my birth father.

The flashback of the strange man suddenly emerging from my memory bank felt significant – as if there was a reason for me not to have mentioned it to Mum all those years back when I was five or six years old. But she never spoke of it again. One thing Mum did later confirm, though, was the tale of my birth father attending my adoption hearing. At the time, the story was a rumour I'd heard from other children and relatives, but at least now I knew it to be true. The fact that Mum was shaken when we'd spoken about the stranger, along with the account of my birth father's appearance in court, makes me believe that the unknown visitor with the machete was actually my birth father. This was my only experience of him and I was never to see or hear of him again.

I've often pleaded with anyone who'd heard a rumour, a whisper, or had a snippet of information to tell me something of what they knew, in the hope that this version at least would be the truth. I've literally begged people for more details, but each time, nobody professed to know anything, effectively shutting me out. Even my mother's best friend, Surinder Auntyji, couldn't tell me anything, having made a promise to my mother many years beforehand – a confidence she wasn't willing to break. Left with no other choice, given no one would speak to me, I resolved to live with my imagination.

What I do know is that Divine intervention was surely at work in that I survived. That took some kind of miracle, in that it was highly unlikely a driver would pull off the road for just one box of fruit. If you saw just one box on its own, you'd most likely assume that it contained fruit that had been rejected or that it was empty and not bother to stop. You'd normally drive on until you came to a pile of boxes, as that denoted a choice of fruits.

But then I may never have been rescued. Or I'd have been found when it was too late – after I'd died from dehydration or hunger. Leopards, hyenas and wild animals would have prowled around and, as scavengers, they'd surely have attacked. I often wonder how abandoned children come to be found. What leads people to discover them? And why them in particular? You read about people who have been found, but what led that person to that exact place?

As to my own background, how did Edgar know to place me there? And what possessed Mr Ozawa to stop when most would have driven past? How was Mr Ozawa guided to find me in such a remote area? What made me silent when I needed to protect myself? How did I manage to stay alive when the odds were against me? How was it that a snake didn't bite me? Was there Divine intervention at hand? The only real explanation? I must have been protected by my guardian angel. Maybe angels had formed a circle around my box, setting up a force field that no animal could penetrate.

While my mum refused to tell me about my origins, when I became a teenager, she did tell me about an extraordinary experience she'd had concerning my adoption. And on this, I do believe every word, because she had absolute faith in the incredible spiritual message that led me into my parents' care.

My parents already had one child, a boy, and Mum was seven months pregnant at the time with my sister, Anju. My mum told me that she started dreaming about me when she became pregnant. She told me that my father would tell her it was all in her imagination, that she was only dreaming of me because of the baby she was already carrying. But, somehow, she knew he was wrong. For in her heart, she just knew that the one she was dreaming about wasn't the one she was expecting – it was me.

She'd explain that my dad was an educated man and that he thought her foolish and fanciful.... But that wasn't the case – she wasn't either of those things. The dreams became more frequent, more intense. And then the goddess Lakshmi began appearing in these dreams, telling my mother about me.

No matter how many times I was told the story of my adoption, I was always fascinated to hear it – of how Goddess Lakshmi had appeared to my mum in a dream to announce my arrival, her most vivid dream yet. Known to lead one to one's goals, the goddess presented an image to Mum of my mum running down a hospital corridor. She told her that I'd be wrapped in a pink blanket and that she'd find me in Kabale Hospital. She even told my mother the number of the ward I'd be in. Knowing the goddess was behind how I came to be part of my adoptive parents' family, I felt truly blessed and special – not knowing then the burden of being the 'chosen' one.

What fascinated me about this story was that both my parents were Sikhs yet revered and respected Hindu beliefs and customs equally. We grew up attending Hindu temples as well as the Gurdwara (Sikh temple). My parents' philosophy tied in with the basic Sikh belief that there is only one God but that God is known by many different names and forms throughout the world.

The next morning, when my mother told my father that I'd arrived and that he was to drive her to Kabale, he articulated, as one might expect, that she was being irrational. So strong was her belief in her dream that she reasoned with him that if I wasn't there, then she'd accept she was nothing but a foolish woman and that the dream was just a figment of her imagination, believing in her heart it would never come to this.

In the end, irritated by Mum's nagging, my father relented on condition she stopped all this nonsense afterwards, agreeing to humour her on this one occasion. Then one last omen was to happen.

Over breakfast on the morning that they were about to leave for the hospital, my dad came across my picture on the front page of the newspaper – the same one Goddess Lakshmi had shown my mother! She couldn't read or write, but she knew. She told me that she took it from him and said, 'Do you believe me now? This is *our* baby. We're going to have a baby girl.'

Mum was heavily pregnant with my younger sister at the time, but she found me exactly as Goddess Lakshmi had said, wrapped in a pink blanket on Ward 21. They fell in love with me instantly and just knew I was to be their daughter.

In 1960s Uganda, there was no such thing as security and people could just walk in and out of hospital at will, but the hospital in Kabale was run by Christian missionaries, who insisted that certain protocols had to be followed. So it was with great disappointment that my parents weren't allowed to take me straight home, though they were allowed to hold me. The equivalent of social services back then was the Save the Children Fund, who had just taken over the case. But unfortunately, the newspaper article stating that an abandoned Asian baby had been found had also invoked dreams of blessings from Goddess Lakshmi for other Asian families. (In the Hindu religion, Goddess Lakshmi bestows success and fortune to those who believe in her.)

A general commotion at the local Save the Children office ensued while they waited for police enquiries to complete, which was difficult when so many other Asian families were coming forward to stake their claim, with Indian couples queuing to have me. But when it was established that I wasn't pure Asian but of mixed heritage – African and Indian – even Goddess Lakshmi couldn't persuade the majority to stay and fight for me, many families falling by the wayside. In the end, only three couples remained at the charity's office.

My mum believed all along that they were meant to have me, for their love was unconditional. I was entrusted to their care as temporary foster carers on 23 September 1960 by the Save the

Children Fund, but she said she just knew in her heart I was meant to be with them and part of their family.

It doesn't appear at the time that there were any in-depth checks as to my adoptive parents' background. We have to remember that this was 1960 at the time and Save the Children Fund were merely interested in securing a loving Asian family to take me in. My understanding is that the only check was my dad's financial stability and his status in the community; he was highly respected.

And their love was unconditional, for while my parents took me in, it was always with the knowledge that if the authorities found my birth mother, I could be returned to her care at any point up until the official adoption, which couldn't take place for six months. At this point, further protocols had to be followed before my official adoption order was eventually granted, on 25 April 1961, placing me in their care permanently. I was officially their daughter.

~

CHAPTER 2

Mixed Blessings

Given my uncertain origins, gossip followed me everywhere:

'Bharti is blessed. The goddess Lakshmi will bless us through her!'

'Thinking of buying a house? Let's get Bharti here. Let Bharti place her hands on the mortgage papers and it'll be ours for sure. Everything will go well....'

'Bharti, can you give us the lottery numbers? We're buying a lottery ticket and we just know the numbers will come up if they come from you.'

My mum's dream-message from Goddess Lakshmi and my subsequent adoption designated me the 'chosen' one. The other couples hoping to adopt me had responded to the newspaper report about my abandonment by a roadside, whereas my illiterate mum always claimed her dream from Goddess Lakshmi came before any official account of my discovery. That the goddess had chosen my mother to have me was surely lucky – and so I came into the world ready-blessed by the deity of motherhood and prosperity herself.

Some weeks after my adoptive parents welcomed me into the family home, my father won the football pools. And that windfall fuelled people's fantasy about me being lucky – not just that I would have a fortunate and prosperous life, but also that I had the power to bestow this luck on anyone else via the goddess herself. I felt no real pressure from my point of view, as I was too young to understand. It was only in my teens that I came to appreciate what this status imposed on me meant, at which point I became torn. It was taken for granted I'd say yes to any request, putting me in a difficult position, a feeling of dread and guilt setting in.

According to some in our local Indian community, an illegitimate child – never mind a child of dual race – should be cast out of society. And so it was that the belief that I'd bring nothing but trouble became intertwined with a golden thread of hope – that, despite my beginnings, I had a role: to make other people rich and lucky, just like my dad.

The amount of money Dad won changed our lives. The win, which was hundreds of thousands of Ugandan shillings, meant Dad was able to have a brand-new house built. And so we moved into a beautiful stone-built dwelling that was large enough for Mum, Dad, us four children and Shiv, my baby brother yet to be born. The new house was next to Dad's garage, Dhir Engineering, and he was able to expand, taking on trainee mechanics, spreading the luck still further in the form of providing jobs and an income for others.

Seeing the material benefits of the pools win for my family sealed my reputation as a 'lucky' child. And that led to many invitations from family, extended family, friends, their friends and virtually anyone else, who would gasp in wonder at the thought that a lucky child like me could bring them wealth.

'Will this house be lucky for us? Well, Bharti is blessed and so Goddess Lakshmi will bless us through her. Everything will go well....'

'Bharti, my wife is pregnant. Please touch her stomach and tell us, is it a boy or a girl? Oh – you don't know. A boy would be good. Perhaps you could just ask God to give us a boy. He'll listen to you.'

'We're moving out of town. Please join us for prayers before we go. If you're there, Goddess Lakshmi will bless us with a safe journey and help us to find prosperity where we're going. You haven't seen any signs that we shouldn't go, have you? Any dreams or nightmares?'

Despite the clamour of demands following me, as a very young child I had no understanding of why I was blessed, or how. How did I know that my father's football pools win had been confirmation that I was indeed very lucky? There were some who envied my parents for adopting me and wished it had been them who had been given that message from the goddess. I was even asked for various blessings by those in the Asian community who had shunned me for being part-African! God certainly had a sense of humour.

I began to feel a sense of importance at being asked to bless this and bless that. Such requests were accompanied by delicious offerings of food and gifts. What child could resist? If there were times when I protested at going on a visit, my brothers and sisters would implore me to go because they'd get a share of the food. We'd have Indian sweets like *laddoos, jalebi* or *gulab jamun*, delicacies that were traditionally offered to celebrate auspicious occasions.

And yet, the light from the attention I enjoyed was to cast a long shadow. As the 'lucky' child, it took me some years to realize that the people who wanted blessings from me didn't see me as worthful. Their eager, expectant looks were tinged with reverence and anxiety – no one wanted me to bless them or their homes half-heartedly – but their expectations began to trigger a deep-seated unease in me as their questions continued:

'Will we be happy here?'

'Will we be rich here?'

'Does this house give you a lucky feeling?'

Suddenly, I became gripped with a sense of fear and foreboding, and I found myself saying 'yes' to every question they asked of me. But then doubts set in. What if that house was unlucky? What if it collapsed on them in an earthquake? I knew the guilt would haunt me for the rest of my life if something went wrong or something bad happened when I'd told them otherwise. I was saying 'yes' to be kind, because I'd learned that the word 'no' made people inconsolable with grief. They'd equate my refusal to answer with that of Goddess Lakshmi refusing to bless them, so strong was their belief in me being her messenger. And I'd just gone along with it all. As just a child, I wouldn't have been free to question them, as that would have been disrespectful, given they were my elders.

With this weight of responsibility came sadness and tears. A lump in my throat would form as thoughts raced around in my head. Then came the realization that I was kidding myself. What I thought was love and acceptance wasn't really that at all. If I wasn't 'lucky', then maybe these people wouldn't give me the time of day under other circumstances. For the sake of wealth and good fortune, they were prepared to overcome their prejudice about me being of mixed race – they appeared to accept *my* colour, when children of dual heritage at that time were often treated with contempt. It was a bitter lesson to learn that, aside from my immediate family, not everyone I knew loved and accepted me for who was; their only interest was in the blessings Goddess Lakshmi would bestow on them if they befriended me or pretended to like me.

I began to understand what true worth meant – and what it didn't.... I had to learn to love myself even when others didn't. The sweets, the biscuits, the reverential treatment meant so little – and from that moment, I trusted only my close family and God, because I knew their love was real and unconditional. Being the lucky child was certainly a mixed blessing, but perhaps I was learning, slowly, how to value myself.

An even greater test of my self-worth was to come.

With my homework book tucked under my arm, I was due to hand over my completed work to the teacher for marking. Standing in the queue at her desk with the other children, it seemed like any other normal day at the missionary school. But when my turn came, she glanced sharply at me, her hand outstretched to take my book. She looked me in the eye and instructed me to wipe my face as there was a mark on it, so I dutifully rubbed it with my hands. Then she frowned and suggested I go to the toilet and check in the mirror.

Off I went, but I could see nothing but my eight-year-old self looking back. Dark brown eyes, curly black hair in plaits, smooth skin. Then I peered more closely: there, on my cheeks, was a colony of tiny clear spots. Miniscule bubbles that hadn't been there earlier – if they had, Anju would have noticed. I couldn't understand how they'd suddenly appeared while I was sitting in class. I thought maybe the bubbles were beads of sweat, but then I wasn't hot. Or maybe they were just water droplets.

I touched one with my fingertip and to my surprise, it felt firm. When I pinched it with my nail, warm, clear liquid trickled onto my cheek and I felt a burning, stinging sensation. The burst bubble was now a tiny flap of skin with a raw, pink mark underneath.

I pinched another one, but the same thing happened. The teacher had insisted I get rid of them, but I couldn't bear the discomfort of popping any more. I dragged my feet back to class, sending up a silent prayer that she'd listen to what I had to say rather than chastise me. I'd need to explain the spots. But how? Surely I must have caused them. There had to be something I'd done. There could be no other explanation – could there?

The teacher looked straight at me when I walked into the classroom. I didn't wait to be asked, instead pre-empting what she might say.

'Miss, I can't do anything with them,' I blurted, my legs shaking.

I was frightened because it looked like I hadn't wiped my face and had deliberately disobeyed her. I was scared she'd scold me in front of the class and that she'd tell my dad, who would surely beat me for not obeying an elder – and a teacher at that.

She instructed me to approach her, concern in her eyes. She took my face in her hands and gently turned my head from side to side, inspecting the tiny pink sores.

'Well I never,' she remarked. 'You need to show your parents.'

My classmates looked at me with curiosity. Anju asked if I might have eaten something to cause it.

'I ate some guavas from the school tree,' I whispered back.

'Oh dear,' she said, all wise. 'That's God's punishment. You know we've been told by the missionary teachers not to steal guavas from that tree.'

Now that was very true. We'd been told in assembly in no uncertain terms that we shouldn't touch the guavas. But of course, being a child, and a bold one at that, I'd climbed the tree and picked some. I'd shared them round and we'd all eaten them – but I was the instigator. The punishment was surely mine. *God is punishing me for eating the guavas!*

I sat in misery, praying and repeatedly apologizing to God for my actions. How was I to know it was such a special tree and that God punished anyone who ate the fruit from it without permission?

Then came another awful realization: worse than God and His punishments was my dad's wrath. If I confessed to eating the forbidden fruit, I'd be in serious trouble for disobeying an order from the school – especially given the teachers were sent by God Himself as missionaries. With this in mind, I decided I couldn't tell him about the spots. Instead, I had to find a way to make them disappear, and fast.

My only option was to keep apologizing to God and never to go near that guava tree again. It was a sombre thought, though, that I was never again to savour that juicy green fruit with its pink seeded flesh, but a promise was a promise. And if God heard me, the spots would surely be gone by the time we sat down to dinner that evening. I believed this with complete conviction, as the Christian teachers had always assured us that whatever we asked for, as long as we held faith in Jesus, it would be granted by God.

At the table that night, I felt really anxious that my parents would see the marks, so I made sure that I sat in a way that the cheek with the most blisters was hidden. There were also a couple of blisters on the other cheek and my forehead, but no one noticed. Anju was the only one at the table who knew, but she didn't spill my secret. After the meal, I scuttled away to my bedroom, hoping against hope that a night's sleep would produce the miracle I needed.

The next morning, I ran to the mirror to see if they'd gone. But I was left in complete shock – the blisters were even bigger, my arms and hands now also covered. They were impossible to hide.

'Anju! Quick. Come in here,' I shouted hysterically.

My sister ran into the bedroom we shared, closing the door tightly behind her at my insistence.

'It's worse!' She couldn't believe what she was seeing, either.

My voice wavered. 'This is some big punishment from God just for eating some guavas! Surely it must be something else.'

'I don't think this is a punishment from God,' Anju said firmly. 'You're going to have to show Dad.'

We both sat on my bed in silence, contemplating his reaction.

I was scared to approach Dad about the blisters, because just a few months before, he'd beaten me severely after he'd seen me laughing with the gardener, assuming it to be flirting, so I knew what he was capable of. I had no idea what I'd done wrong at the time and Dad had never laid a finger on me before, so the beating had come as a shock. I'd been playing hide-and-seek outside and the gardener had pointed to a good hiding place. I'd smiled, said thank you and hidden. That was all.

After we'd finished playing our game, my father had beckoned me over to him. Something in his gaze made me nervous and I hid behind my mum, holding on to her *kameeze* (tunic). Mum implored him not to hit me, protesting that I was just a child. I saw the bat raised in his hand. Mum put herself in his way in an attempt to stop him from getting hold of me, but in a matter of seconds, he'd grabbed my arm and yanked me away from Mum.

I was unable to break free and he was raining blows all over me. Warm liquid trickled down my face and Mum started screaming at him to stop it, saying he was going to kill me. She pulled me away from him and tried to shield me once more. But he was having none of it, a determination about him that I'd never seen before. He seemed intent on doing just that – killing me.

I could feel my siblings' eyes bearing down on us from the veranda. Frozen to the spot, they were no doubt too scared to come to my aid. All the house servants had gathered to see what was happening. They called out to Dad to stop hurting me, but not one of the adults stepped forwards to protect me. I was terrified and felt humiliated, my pain clear for all to see.

Suddenly, I was on the floor. I could hear screaming – mine – and my voice begging Dad to stop as I curled into a ball in shock while he continued to thrash me.

'I'll teach you *never* to smile at the gardener again if it's the last thing I do!' Dad shouted. 'How dare you bring disgrace to this family!'

I must have turned my head from the floor at one point, because I witnessed the gardener fleeing from the house as he rushed through the gate and into the garden. He looked alarmed. Maybe he thought he'd be beaten next.

Then my mother came running from the kitchen with a knife. 'You hit her once more,' she cried, 'and you'll see me dead.' She held the point of the knife to her stomach. 'Do. It. Once. More. And. I. Die.'

I was terrified that she meant every word, that his actions would seal her fate. But the bat thudded onto the veranda floor.

'Do you know her?' He pointed down at me, full of contempt. 'Is she worth fighting for? Is it worth turning against me?'

The house fell silent.

'Mark my words, she'll bring you nothing but shame and dishonour. This girl you're saving will one day be the cause of your death and our family's shame.'

'I don't care,' Mum wept. 'She's my daughter, my beloved daughter.' She cradled me, wiping the blood from my head with her *chunni* (scarf).

Everyone melted away. The ayah (nanny) fetched a bowl of water and cotton wool, weeping silently with Mum as they tended to my cuts and bruises. From that night, my mother slept in my bed, refusing to speak to my father.

Girls and women in Indian society were treated so differently from the boys and men. We'd be told not to sit with our legs parted, yet I'd see my brother with his legs sprawled and think there was one rule for them and one for us. We were even told not to laugh raucously, because if we laughed too loudly, we weren't deemed to be ladylike. Only bad women laughed out loud and opened their mouths wide enough to show their teeth. But then, how can you laugh with your mouth closed? I'd wonder at that, until one day I noticed women did so shielded behind their hands, or that they covered their mouths with their *chunnis* almost in embarrassment – especially if men were around. Men had no problem with laughter, though, and my dad and brother could laugh loudly and freely, slapping their thighs.

When male relatives came to visit, my parents would make my sister and me cover our heads as young girls. And when we were older, not only did we have to cover our heads, but we also had to wear dresses below the knee and tops long enough to cover our backsides.

When a 'whistling' craze swept the school, everyone tried to learn to whistle, but as girls we were forbidden from doing so. Whistling was considered unladylike, and again, only girls or women who were considered improper did such base things as whistle.

Girls were given lectures on many occasions as to how they could and couldn't behave, and I felt a real sense of injustice about these rules as a child. This was my sense of worth rising to the surface.

It comes with anger, and it comes from injustice. As girls, that was another thing we weren't supposed to show, either: anger. But I felt it nonetheless and came to recognize it as my worth letting me know whenever a situation just wasn't right. That feeling of worth always began with an emotion, not a thought. I'd feel it first in the pit of my stomach and then it would rise into my heart. Even in those early years it became my form of protection from subservience to rules I didn't understand or believe in.

When my brother's friends came to play, they'd say a quick hello but always stayed apart from us. That's the way we were all brought up – not only our family, but also everyone we knew. One of our relatives even segregated his sons and daughters in different parts of their house. The boys were all kept in one quarter and across the veranda in the other quarter were the girls, who were only allowed to join their siblings at mealtimes.

When men came to the house, the girls were expected to make a quick exit – my elder brother could stay, though. The women would go into one room, the men into another. When relatives or friends came, the boys and men ate first. Girls and women ate last, and sometimes ended up with just scraps.

Even now, when I visit certain relatives for a big gathering, men and women are shown into separate rooms. First the men are fed, then the children, and the women eat last – nothing having changed in all these years. My worth still tells me to question why, as a woman, I should be of least importance. But then why should anyone be last, for that matter?

I noticed that some of my female cousins weren't allowed to eat meat or eggs, but their brothers could. I later came to understand that these foodstuffs were thought to be heat-producing and therefore likely to bring on early menstruation. Another explanation was the belief that these foods may make a girl have lustful thoughts, as these foods were thought to heat the blood. However, it was fine for boys and men to have 'hot blood' and be lustful in their behaviour. How could this be right?

When laughing with the gardener and making eye contact that day, I was deemed to have broken the rules. Looking back, I know if my sisters had done the same thing, there would still have been consequences, but my transgression had an even deeper meaning and a greater punishment. It was as if Dad had acted out every ounce of negativity he'd been forced to absorb from the town, from those relatives who didn't agree with my adoption and from those who thought I should have been left to die on the roadside from dehydration or prowling wildcats.

In Hinduism there's the idea of karma, an inherited life path. People actually said to my face that I'd get pregnant and have an illegitimate baby like my birth mother did. They believed in all honesty that because my biological mother did it, it meant I had the same dirty blood inside me, therefore standing to reason I was going to do the same thing, in their eyes.

When my dad saw that interaction between myself and the gardener, I believe it triggered a moment of madness in him. That huge cultural pressure that girls shouldn't shame themselves or their entire families by looking at men, plus the negativity about me being adopted, erupted into a fury that was later to ravage him with guilt.

And yet, what my parents did, taking me in, was actually not only an extraordinary act, but also a courageous one – to take me in when the messages around them, the predictions about my future, were so dire. Dad fought off that negativity from the second they brought me home from the hospital. He didn't adopt me because he thought I'd bring him luck – he adopted me because Mum told him that Goddess Lakshmi had said, 'You've got to have this child.' They had such faith that they were doing the right thing.

I know my dad loved me – he loved all of us, my brothers and my sisters included – but the moment he raised the weapon to me, societal influence won. It was his way of holding his hands up and saying, 'I've made a mistake.' Everybody had told him I was going to bring dishonour on the family. They said I had dirty blood, which meant that I was going to do what my birth mother had done and give birth to an illegitimate child, like she had. As a teenager, it was almost expected by some relatives that I'd have a baby out of wedlock – the ultimate shame brought upon a family culturally – and now I'd proven them right by my own actions. They might as well have been saying, 'Look, I've just seen her flirting with the gardener.' The evidence was right there, the proof that I'd gone the same way as my birth mother. At just eight years old.

The beating also proved to me beyond doubt that the adoption story was true – even though my parents had done their utmost to keep it a secret from me. So, ultimately, if Dad had hoped to maintain that secret, the beating and his accompanying words were certain indicators that I wasn't family. Why else would he have beaten me for no good reason? It was because I'd brought shame on them.

A few weeks before that terrible day, I'd found myself looking up the word 'adoption' in the dictionary, having crept into Dad's study one morning when no one was around. I was an avid reader and I'd read all the books in the house. My father used to read *Reader's Digest* magazines and sometimes I'd read them, too. I knew that we were forbidden to go in his study, but that morning when I saw my chance, I'd pushed open the study door, hoping to find one in his desk. Instead, what I found astounded me and was to change my life as I knew it forever. It would also bring about a greater understanding of some of the reasons I was different, for on the desk was a folder with my name on it, inside of which were newspaper cuttings and the judge's ruling on my adoption.

I now believe I was guided to enter the study that morning. I was steered there because it was time I knew the truth.

I opened the dictionary and read: *'Adoption. Legally taking another's child and bringing it up as one's own.'* I didn't understand at first. Dad used to say that I looked like him. It was a game we'd play on a Sunday. Mum would grab hold of my sister Anju and brother Shankerdas and say that they looked like her, at which point Dad would grab hold of me and my younger sister, Mina, and say that we looked just like him. Funnily enough, I never saw a difference between my looks and those of my siblings until I came to understand what the word 'adoption' meant.

At school, though, children would casually remark that Mum and Dad weren't my real parents. I'd hit out at them and they'd repeat it, fuelling the situation. I was always getting into fights, proclaiming that what they were saying wasn't true, believing them just to be the cruel taunts of children. My father used to tell me to ignore them, always pointing out how much alike we looked, refuting their claims.

But the truth was that my dad didn't look like me at all. My parents and their friends had occasionally spoken in code around me and I overheard snippets of unfinished conversations to which I wasn't privy, like 'that other couple wanted her, too…' and 'her real father couldn't have her…'. I realize now they must have been discussing how I came to be adopted. But then, we were just children, adding two plus two and coming up with eight, in our attempts to make sense of what was being said. When they were talking, I'd be in the room, craving to understand what they meant and what they were referring to, listening in. When they realized, they'd make me sit elsewhere, waving me to the far side of the room, or out of the room altogether. I knew there was a secret about me. Something wasn't right.

That day, I dropped the file back on Dad's desk and ran to find Anju, saying, 'You'll never believe it. You know all those kids at school who said that I'm not your real sister? Well, they're telling the truth.'

'What do you mean?'

'Well, I found this file…'.

After I'd explained, her first words were, 'Why did you go in Dad's study? Why? You know we're not allowed in there!'

I, too, was terrified, because there would be big trouble if anyone found out I'd been in the study.

'Yeah, but don't you see? It says that I'm adopted.'

'What does that even mean?' she asked.

I told Anju that it meant I'd come from somebody else, from elsewhere. She asked me to show her, so we darted into the study and I produced the file.

'Well, it doesn't really matter, does it, because you *are* my sister. We're just going to have to pretend we don't know about this. It changes nothing between us.'

I agreed, more afraid of the consequences of going into a forbidden room than what would happen if my parents found out what I'd discovered about my birth. As it is with other families, there's often a tacit understanding that some things will never be discussed.

Sadly, my first and only beating from my dad wasn't the end of the matter, for he approached me one day and took me to one side, the coldness of his expression so grave that I expected to be beaten again. Instead, he merely informed me that I wasn't going to school that day and that there was a visitor coming to see me. I was mystified. Who was this person? It had been a week or so since the beating, and in that time Dad hadn't spoken a word to me. I'd assumed it to be part of my punishment, nothing more.

I turned to Mum, but her face was set rigid.

'It. Is. Not. Happening.' She gritted her teeth, glaring at my father. 'If it does, I will never, *ever* forgive you. Never!'

I was confused, not understanding a word of what they meant or to what they were referring.

The visitor was a Mr Johnson, and when he arrived he spent ages with my father. He looked kind and I took to him instantly. He apologized for keeping me so long and I mentioned that Mr Johnson was lucky Dad was able to see him for so long, as he was usually a very busy man. Then he touched my arm, noticing the purple bruising. He asked me what had happened and how I'd come to hurt myself.

'I got beaten for being naughty.' My voice was steady, clear.

As far as I was concerned, I was just relating the facts. In Africa, children got beaten all the time – at school, at home, by neighbours. Any adult could raise a hand to a child and parents accepted that the adult was right to do so – that the child must have done something wrong to have received a beating and therefore deserving of the treatment.

He asked me what I'd done and I told him about the incident with the gardener. I explained that it was my fault and that I shouldn't have spoken to him or hidden where he told me to, and that my father wasn't to blame for his actions. I surprised myself at the tears welling and how my voice was shaking with the injustice of it all; knowing I was taking my father's side and blaming myself for the beating, but in my heart I did not accept I had done anything wrong.

Mr Johnson looked over my shoulder towards Dad.

'Did you hear that, Mr Chand? Your daughter's just explained what *actually* happened.'

His tone was accusatory, and I turned to see my father, pale and silent.

'See what you've done?' I whispered to Mr Johnson. 'Now I'm going to get another beating, for sure.'

'No, you won't. I promise.'

Mr Johnson's tone was certain. I believe I saw anger on his face, just for a second, but then decided I'd imagined it.

'Tell me about the book you're reading,' he asked, sitting further forwards.

'It's called *The Secret Garden*. I love reading. I've read nearly all the books in school.'

'It sounds like your life is happy,' he said. 'Are you? Happy, I mean.'

'Of course I'm happy,' I said. 'I have the best mum and dad in the world. And I love my sisters and brother. We do lots of things together.'

'Tell me, what does your daddy do to make you happy?'

'He takes us on safaris. He's shown us how to shoot so we can defend ourselves if a wild animal comes along. He makes sausages for breakfast. He buys us lovely toys and books. He's very caring....'

'And your mother? What does your mum do to make you happy?' Mr Johnson asked.

'She makes the best food.' I pointed to my flowery dress. 'My mum made this. She knits also. Best of all... she gives me lots of hugs and kisses.' Then I lowered my voice. 'She's furious with Dad for hitting me. She sleeps with me and holds me all night now.' I looked round, anxious that no one should overhear. 'I'm her special daughter. She really, really loves me.'

At that moment, my sisters and brother came running in from

school. Anju gave me a hug.

'I missed you today!' she said.

'This is Mr Johnson,' I said importantly. 'He's come to ask us if we're happy at home.'

I'd included my sister, as I'd assumed he was going to ask my siblings if they were happy, too. I had no idea then that he'd been summoned by my dad.

'Of course we are!' Anju giggled. 'What a silly question.'

Mr Johnson didn't speak to me again until the end of the day, instead watching me play with my sisters and Shankerdas, read aloud and practise my recorder. Every now and then, I noticed he wrote notes.

Mr Johnson sat with us at the dinner table. My father had slumped in moody silence and I sat as far away from him as possible in case he hit me again. I'd not forgotten he'd overheard what I'd said about the gardener.

After dinner, Mr Johnson approached us children and shook our hands.

'Thank you all for letting me share such a wonderful day with you,' he said.

I remember being amazed. An adult thanking a child was unheard of. Mr Johnson drew me aside and gave me a card.

'I work for the Save the Children Fund,' he said quietly. 'If you're ever upset or sad, just call me and I'll visit you to make sure everything's all right.'

Later, I heard muted voices from the sitting room.

'If I'd taken her with me today, I'd have destroyed her trust in people forever,' Mr Johnson was saying.

My father murmured something and I heard Mr Johnson say, 'It's too late. Where will she go? Who will look after her? If you do this, you'll shatter her little life for good.'

There was a note of irritation in his voice. I could see my mum sitting on the sofa, not saying a word. She looked angry and anxious. Over dinner, I noticed she'd been tense. She didn't even smile or speak to Mr Johnson. It wasn't like her to be rude to a guest.

Mr Johnson's voice rose a little when he spoke next.

'But if you *ever* beat her again in the way you did, Mr Chand, I'll personally see to it that she does leave here, make no mistake.'

My father could be heard muttering his apologies over and over – I believe they were sincere.

Curious as ever, my siblings wanted to know what they were discussing. I told them I thought it was about me and they didn't question it further. Not that I could have answered, as I didn't really understand myself, other than that my father had asked Mr Johnson to take me somewhere and that my mother was against it.

What had the Save the Children Fund got to do with me? Why was there talk of me being taken away? And who was Mr Johnson to tell my father off? I suddenly felt angry that my father was being made to apologize – and for what? Teaching me right from wrong? I pulled the card Mr Johnson had given me from my pocket and tore it into pieces. I'd never call him, I decided. Not if he was going to send me away....

My poor mum had had no say in the matter whatsoever. Even though she'd asserted to my dad all those years ago that she was going to have this baby – me – no matter what she said now, it made no difference. Even though it had been Goddess Lakshmi's express wishes back then, when it came to Dad having doubts about me now, there was nothing she could do. Dad had overruled her and invited Mr Johnson into our home. She was powerless in that particular situation. But Mr Johnson's word would overrule Dad's wild theory that maybe society was right.

Dad might have thought he was protecting the family honour by having me removed and placed elsewhere, but this man's word would be final and Dad would have no say in the matter. I had no idea where I'd have been taken if I'd been forced to go. The incident with the gardener was just a warning sign of the gradual erosion of my worth. From that moment, an element of self-doubt started to creep in about who I was and where I belonged.

Looking back, it seems to me Dad was in a state of confusion – a definite conflict was going on in his mind as he contemplated his love for me versus the demonic predictions coming true about me turning out like my birth mother. But I came to believe he didn't want me to go, didn't want Mum to be upset. While worrying about the future, he hadn't understood the consequences of my being removed, not just on me, but also the rest of my family. My father was held in high regard for going against the norm and adopting me despite misgivings. But my removal would have been something that would have had ramifications for not only the family, but also his standing in the community. Fear of others' predictions had made him irrational – I was just a child. Mr Johnson's visit had really brought home the consequences of any removal, making Dad focus on what his actions would mean. But after that, I became so ill that beatings were furthest from their minds.

During that time, I began to feel a sense of uncertainty about my life, my identity and my sense of belonging. As a child in the Uganda of the 1960s, the existing parental culture further undermined my already unsteady sense of self. Alongside the restrictions on girls' behaviour, there was a further decree that applied to all of us without exception, whereby parents threatened to dispose of their children so casually. It was commonplace to have children sent away to orphanages or to relatives on the other side of the country or the world, the threat to kill them ever-present. It was standard for parents to warn, 'I brought you into this world and I can take you out of it just as easily.'

At that time, children were brought into a life of love alongside the harsh reality of actual physical beatings, where they'd live in fear of being thrashed. And as a child, you were convinced that an adult both could and would kill you, such was the unbearable rule of discipline in even the most loving of families.

It was usual for a child to come into school and say, 'Dad broke my finger' or, 'My mum hit me with a stick yesterday.' And if you were beaten at school with a stick, you didn't dare go home and say anything, because you'd be beaten once again for being beaten in the first place, the reasoning being that you surely did something wrong to warrant the beating at all – a kind of reinforcement of the original punishment.

When Dad beat me that terrible day, some boys in the town who were friends with my brother came up to me saying they'd heard I'd been chastised and that not even they'd had it so harsh. I almost smile now to think of how I'd climbed the school hierarchy because of this incident. Kudos at last.

———

So there I was, thinking about the potential beating that was sure to come and looking at the spots that had erupted all over me overnight.

'I don't think I should tell Dad about the guavas,' I said tentatively, hoping my sister would agree.

'You're right. There's no need. I don't think it's the guavas, anyway. We all steal them, but have you seen any other child at school get a reaction?'

'True!'

Sweet relief. Maybe I was wrong, after all. Maybe it wasn't God punishing me. A feeling of hope resonated in my heart.

My dad was reading the newspaper out on the veranda and I approached him timidly. At first he didn't acknowledge my presence, barely having spoken to me since Mr Johnson's departure.

'Daddyji, I need you to look at what's happened to me!' I said urgently.

He put down his newspaper and a ripple of shock spread over his face as he finally glanced up.

'What happened?' He'd gently taken my arms. 'You're covered in blisters.' He'd reached out and touched one on my face. 'When did this happen? They look like burns. Have you burned yourself?'

I told him the story.

'Why didn't you show me yesterday?'

I wanted to say that I was worried in case he hit me again, but those words didn't come. Instead, I said, 'I thought the blisters would disappear and I didn't want to worry you or Mummyji.'

My father hugged me for the first time in ages. 'You shouldn't keep something like this to yourself.'

Things moved fast after that. Dr Desai came to the house and examined me. It seemed I had blisters everywhere, and some were so big that they'd burst and left sore patches on my skin. The doctor vowed to return that afternoon, needing to research my symptoms, having never seen anything like it. He also cautioned my father not to let me play out in the sun, believing the heat would aggravate the condition. Dr Desai didn't return that afternoon, instead calling to say that he was still trying to identify what I had but that he'd visit the following day.

So that was it – no playing outside.

That night, Dad insisted the fans stay on – my room might have been cool but I was left shivering.

When I awoke the next morning, to my surprise, the bedclothes were hurting me and I tried to pull them off, but the fabric was stuck to my sores. I started wailing and my parents ran in. It was my father who fetched a bowl of warm water and wads of cotton wool. He soaked the fabric where it was glued to me and gently began to peel the bedding off me.

Dr Desai arrived with ointment, bandages and special gauze designed not to stick to the sores. He told my father of a condition called epidermolysis bullosa. Pronouncing those two words was beyond me at the time, but later I'd have to learn how – as it was to remain with me forever. My illness could be controlled with steroids, Dr Desai explained, but there was no cure. The words 'no cure' hung in the air, but Dad chose to ignore them.

Dad refused to let steroids be administered. The list of side effects – delayed growth, weakened bones, aggressive mood swings, increased appetite leading to weight gain – were too much of a risk for an eight-year-old. Instead, he resolved to seek out alternative methods of treatment from the best skin specialists in the world. It became apparent that he'd try anything.

Our travels were about to begin.

~

CHAPTER 3

Specialist Doctors of Uganda

'How dare you pinch my daughter deliberately! Can't you see you're hurting her, you imbecile!'

The student doctors' eyes widened in disbelief as my father punched the prominent specialist in the face.

Dad turned to me. 'Get your clothes on, we're leaving. No, don't bother. Put your dressing gown on – we're going now.'

And that was the end of my stay at Mulago National Specialised Hospital in Kampala, our capital city.

It had begun when Dad had heard about a Dr H, a prominent specialist doctor in Uganda – a Westerner who specialized in treating rare skin diseases. Dad had driven me all the way to Mulago from our little town of Kabale, some 400 kilometres or so (250 miles), thinking this esteemed doctor might have the answers. They'd admitted me on arrival and there we were, full of hope, with me propped up on clean sheets waiting for the famous Dr H to appear.

The fracas had started when Dr H had inserted a needle into my blisters to draw out the fluid and take it away for testing. As he did so, the blisters popped and seeped, the needle pricking the raw wounds underneath. Over the next few days, he'd taken pieces of skin, too – from the underside of the blisters on my left knee, from my cheek, from my wrists and from the backs of my hands. Afterwards, I'd needed stitches, but when he cut the flesh from my cheek, it was agony. He called them biopsies and told me that they were designed to help them see what was happening to my skin in the hope of finding a cure.

I felt like I shouldn't complain, but the pain left me little choice. Dad seemed unconvinced that all was well and on this particular day had resolved to visit during a ward round to see what was happening for himself. He sat beside me and stayed quiet, but I knew he was all eyes when Dr H and his students had gathered around my bed with their white coats and clipboards. *A flock of birds waiting to feed on me*, I thought at the time.

I'd found myself shaking on the inside when Dr H had located a patch of clear skin on the back of my hand. He'd pinched it and twisted sharply, a new blister popping up in an instant as he demonstrated what happens with this condition to his students. But it hurt. *It really hurt.*

By the time he did it a second time, I was crying. But he wouldn't get a third chance.

The students had stood open-mouthed as my dad had punched the eminent doctor in the face, Dr H left staggering backwards, holding his cheek in shock. Dad had grabbed my case and we more or less ran from the ward to the car. Dad was tall and raced ahead, leaving me stumbling and wincing behind him, struggling to keep up.

We headed to a friend of Dad's, who lived near Kampala. I walked into the house in my dressing gown and their daughters-in-law helped me to change into my clothes. They looked at my cheek, at the marks that are still visible even to this day. Five hours later, we were home. When I saw Mum waiting for us on the veranda, I sobbed with relief.

Dad striking the specialist became big news – and it seemed that news travelled far and wide, as we tried one doctor after another, only to find that no one would see me after that. As soon as we turned up at a hospital and gave our names, they'd mention the incident and refuse to see us.

In the end, Dad heard about a Dr S in Kampala, a renowned skin specialist, and decided he wanted him to see me, hoping desperately that he wouldn't refuse like the others. Dad phoned him incessantly until eventually he reluctantly agreed to see us.

When we arrived, Dr S's first words to us were, 'You've dropped like a stone on my head.' (In Uganda, that means you're not welcome as you've turned up uninvited.) 'You've disrespected a very good friend of mine, Dr H, and then you come here.... If he can't help you, what makes you think I can? I suggest you leave now. I never want to see you or your daughter again.'

I felt sorry for my father. No one had ever dared speak to him in that way and I was sad that my blisters had led to this.

Dad was on his feet.

'I'm sorry you feel that way,' he began, his voice shaking with rage. 'But I'm not sorry I hit your friend. He pinched my daughter to see how the blisters formed merely in demonstration for his students so they could learn. His actions caused yet another unnecessary blister and more pain for my daughter. I defy you to show me any father who will stand by and watch their child cry out without intervening.

'I came to you in the hope that you'd see my daughter and witness her suffering. I mistakenly thought that you'd care more about helping her, what with the wonderful reputation you have, but clearly your friendships mean more.'

We were walking out of the room as my father spoke. At the door, Dad turned and faced Dr S.

'And you could have told me all that over the phone. We've travelled six hours for this, causing great discomfort for my daughter.'

I could tell my father was badly affected by this whole episode, as he turned to me in the car and said, 'We think these white doctors are gods, but they're just arrogant bastards who look down on us because of the colour of our skin. They're not interested in helping at all.'

I was both shocked and elated at the same time. It was unusual for Dad to speak ill of people, but he'd also spoken to me like an adult for the first time.

Later, a letter came from Dr S apologizing for his actions, having since confirmed with Dr H what he'd done to me. He invited my father back for a consultation and gave us the name of a Dr Emerson, a skin specialist in England, whom he was sure would help. Dad decided this would be our next move: a visit to England. But we'd have to save up for that. What I didn't know then was that Dr Emerson *would* come into my life, but not in the way you'd think. I was to see him three years later – and without my father's intervention.

In the meantime Dr Desai, our family doctor, prescribed a new medicine, a steroid called prednisone. Despite that, my condition remained as chronic as ever. My father insisted I took the smallest dose to avoid the potential side effects. As you already know, there was no known treatment that worked, which wasn't surprising given so few people had experience in treating my particular rare illness, but at least the steroids alleviated it somewhat.

I had blisters everywhere: in my mouth, on my scalp, on the soles of my feet. I couldn't chew, let alone wash or comb my hair, and I couldn't walk, either. In bed, the blister fluid and blood seeped into the sheets, meaning Mum had to soak the sheets in warm water each morning to unstick me really gently. It was either that or my skin would peel off and bleed again, which was excruciatingly painful.

Endless days and nights were spent lancing blisters once they were 'ready'. Every time I bumped myself even slightly, either my skin peeled off or a blister formed. I also lost all the nails on my right hand and on my toes. I was reassured that they'd grow back one day, but they never did, the nail beds completely destroyed by the epidermolysis bullosa. Being right-handed, my right hand had got knocked a lot more than my left and any disturbance to the skin had resulted in a blister. If a blister came up under the nail, it pushed the nail off.

I felt dirty and sticky, and my skin felt like it was on fire. In school assemblies, the missionaries might talk about heaven and hell – hell being depicted as hot and for bad people, as we all know. We'd had it drummed into us that if we didn't believe in Jesus and the one true God, then there would be consequences.... Was this the consequence of my own disbelief?

The missionaries were very kind to us, but when I was in pain, I could only think about that hellfire and damnation they spoke of. The teachers didn't need to remind me about hell – I felt I was already there. I often thought my illness was a punishment from God for not becoming a Christian, so I'd offer my prayers to Jesus and pray to Him, telling Him that I did believe in Him. Then I'd ask God to make me better – all to no avail.

Dad kept hoping Dr Desai's medication would work, but we still spent every weekend travelling here and there between specialists. Just Dad and me, in our futile attempt to find a doctor to heal my raging skin. We had lots of names to work through and my father was determined to visit every single one on his list, no matter how far we had to travel. In the past, on Saturdays, Dad's garage was always open, but once the blisters came, everything changed. He'd close the garage or leave an employee in charge so the two of us could continue our quest.

I loved those journeys when it was just the two of us. Dad always took time to stop if he spotted an animal in the distance. He saw so much without the need for binoculars and I never ceased to be amazed at how he could see lions or leopards shielding from the heat in a tree as if he had X-ray vision. We'd stop to watch dik-diks, small relatives of the antelope, or warthogs or elephants. Dad would hold the binoculars gently to my eyes, making sure they didn't rest on my nose, as their weight would have caused my skin to tear. Then he'd point to where the animals were hiding, grazing or running.

Sometimes we'd see boxes on the side of the road and there would be mangoes, guavas, melons or bananas for sale. On sounding the car horn to announce our presence, we'd wait patiently for the farmer to arrive, whereupon Dad would buy whatever it was that I wanted to eat and we'd be off again, munching some succulent piece of fruit on our way.

We'd travel for hours, sometimes getting up in the early hours of the morning to make the journey, only for the specialist to take one look at me and shake his head. The consultation was often over in an instant. Some doctors and healers were even afraid to shake my father's hand, in case they caught my disease from him, believing in their ignorance that maybe he was infected but not yet showing symptoms. Others simply refused to let me step out of the car, again thinking I was contagious. They'd peer through the car window yelling, 'Take her away! Get her away from here,' flapping their arms at me until Dad slammed his hand on the steering wheel and drove off.

Now I shouldn't have been shocked at this, because the idea of me being contagious wasn't new. Whenever we visited relatives, some of the aunties, uncles and cousins refused to hug me. They'd embrace my sisters and brother in front of me, all smiles, while choosing to ignore me – and how that hurt! At mealtimes, they'd give me a different plate – often a different colour or size so it could be recognized easily. Once, I even heard my aunty whisper to my cousin, 'Make sure you wash that separately.' Similarly, some went so far as to put the plate and glass I'd used in the bin, believing that even washing it wouldn't protect them from contamination. Thankfully, not all of my relatives or family friends treated me that way. Some of them gave me extra hugs and the same kind of plate as everyone else.

The rejection I felt had started well before my illness, though. Some relatives didn't accept me simply because I was adopted and of mixed race. I wasn't 'their blood'. Not only was I Asian–African, but I was also someone's abandoned child, which meant I had no place in the family. Back then, they showed their true feelings by not greeting me or looking at me, focusing instead on my siblings and parents. Some looked straight through me, and if they embraced me, I sensed that it was perfunctory and meaningless. Even today, some people are polite to my face, but still I sense their disapproval and rejection. As a child, this rejection really hurt. I'd well up with tears but pretend nothing was wrong. So when even the doctors, whose job it was to heal, treated me like I was contagious, all the hurt from those visits to relatives came flooding back, opening yet more raw wounds.

Some of these doctors took money from my father in advance. That's when I learned a new word from Dad. Well, two new words: bastard quacks. I had no idea what he meant, but I heard it many times on our journeys together. I began to realize it wasn't a compliment when after yet another wasted journey, I shouted, 'Bastard quacks!' just like he did. But Dad firmly told me these were words only adults used and that he never wanted to hear me saying them again – especially not a lady. After that, he resorted to muttering it under his breath, realizing how impressionable I was, and when he was really frustrated, he changed it to 'Bloody rascals.'

One doctor became my favourite for a week or two, because his advice was to drink two litres of ice-cold water with glucose powder stirred in as many times a day as I could manage. His opinion was that my body was burning up from the inside, which was why my skin burned on the outside. The cooling drink administered daily was thought to soothe the blisters in my mouth and 'douse the heat inside me'. It was always hot in the car and I loved that sugary drink. I also loved the idea of it putting out the flames curling up inside my tummy. You can imagine my disappointment when, no doubt thousands of shillings later, the doctor declared he couldn't understand why the remedy wasn't working.

'Maybe,' he said, looking at me darkly, 'just maybe your daughter is eating the foods I forbade. Are you eating mangoes?'

I shook my head dolefully. I loved mangoes, but I knew they were forbidden, as they were a 'heat-producing food'. Tomatoes, guavas, meat, okra, anything cooked with onions and bitter gourd were all deemed to be heat-producing foods. (I hated bitter gourd anyway, so it was a great excuse not to have it.)

Once he'd finished with his questions, he wrote out his invoice for thousands of shillings and said he knew the name of another doctor who might be able to help, effectively washing his hands of me – but not the lure of money. So the following weekend, off we went again.

This next doctor said I was to drink raw bitter gourd juice to cleanse my blood. That didn't last long. It didn't matter how much sugar was added, I just couldn't do it. Thousands of shillings later, the doctor said he couldn't help because the sugar was contaminating the juice, so it wouldn't cleanse the blood. He was severe in his telling-off, asking if I was really interested in being cured.

My brother, Shankerdas, and sister Anju joined me in one of these quests for a cure. This doctor, a Doctor P, lived in a mansion perched on a hill near Jinja, 70 kilometres (40 miles or so) west of the capital, Kampala, which was the farthest we'd ever been before. From Dr P's front garden, we could see all the hills and mountains beyond, with a river coursing its way through the valley below. We were beside ourselves with excitement, pointing and jumping at the sight of hippos wading in the river and real crocodiles basking on rocks. *Wow – what a view!*

But they took me inside straight away. I wasn't allowed out in the sun, as the heat made the blisters worse, so Dad and I were led from the garden into a room that didn't even have a window to gaze out of. In the space of just a minute, I'd left behind all the sunshine and fun – the story of my life....

Time was definitely on this doctor's side. He asked what felt like hundreds of questions and it seemed we'd been there for hours. I could hear Anju and Shankerdas playing outside and wondered when I could join them, even just for a short time – or at least watch. Dad could have answered all the questions without me being there in that gloomy office.

I wanted to ask this doctor a few things myself. Like, had a crocodile ever climbed up to his house? How did the electric fence keep all the animals out? Had any animal tried to get in? Can crocodiles jump? I also thought about barbeques and how all the animals might come charging up to eat. These questions stayed in my head, but I was dying to ask.

Then came the 20-minute 'treatment', during which I was told to sit in a metal contraption that encased me right up to my neck. The bench inside it was wooden. I sat gingerly on the edge, as I had sores on the backs of my thighs. It was a deep-steam treatment designed to 'draw out all of my impurities'. The doors were bolted on the outside and there was no way I could get out.

I've never experienced pain like it. Already in agony from the sores, it felt like boiling water was being poured on my wounds.

My howls of pain brought Shankerdas and Anju running inside. They stopped in shock when they saw me, just my head sticking out from the steam torture chamber. I begged them to let me out.... Tears of panic were threatening and I didn't know how much longer I could stand it.

'The pain is due to the impurities being drawn out of her body,' said Dr P as he shooed my brother and sister away. 'You must all ignore her screams and cries – it's for her own good.'

Dad's expression was one of worry. He was clearly scared, but then his face changed. He set his chin firm and I knew he didn't want to hear my cries of protestation. After all, he'd been told Dr P was the best-ever prominent alternative specialist doctor in Uganda. This treatment would surely be 'the' one.

Dr P eventually let me out of the steam cabinet. I looked like I'd been scalded in a fire, my skin red raw, blisters forming on top of blisters. *There was no way I was coming back here.* Bits of my skin were strewn all over the cabinet seat.

After a nurse had helped me to dress, I said in my loudest voice, 'You know those bastard quacks you talk about, Daddyji?' I didn't wait for his answer. 'Well, this bastard quack has charged you the most and he's the worst of the lot. I wouldn't waste any more money on him.'

I gave Dr P a smile and almost laughed at both his and Dad's expressions. Holding my dress as far away from me as I could so it didn't stick to my raw skin, I hobbled and winced all the way to the car. Inside, I sat forwards with my forehead on the seat in front trying to ease off my dress, the fabric sticking fast to the gaping sores on my stomach, chest, back and buttocks. Although I had blisters on my face, my forehead was the only part of me where the skin hadn't peeled off and where I felt relative comfort. Blood seeped into my clothes and the car seat, but the thought of Dr P's face and me calling him a bastard quack kept me laughing away the pain.

Dad thought the treatment had sent me mad, because I kept laughing all the way home. Every time I giggled, he'd give me a sideways look, clearly concerned. There was a woman in town who wandered around laughing at nothing and having a private conversation with herself – it must have seemed to him that the extent of his daughter's pain had turned her mad, too.

I, on the other hand, decided the pain was worth it, as that was the most I'd laughed in ages. And the best part? I never got scolded for what I'd said, or for laughing! Dad must have thought that a telling-off on top of everything would have tipped me over the edge, but I did overhear him telling Mum how embarrassed he'd been. I really hoped that feeling of humiliation would stop him from taking me back to Dr P any time soon.

It was at least eight weeks before I was well enough to go back to the mansion on the hill. Mum begged Dad not to take me back. Even my brother and sister refused to come this time, because they couldn't bear the thought of listening to my screams. So it was just me and Dad again, back on the road to Jinja, then into that windowless office with the crocodiles waiting below. It didn't cross my mind to throw myself to their mercy, but I remember thinking I might well make a run for it and let the electric fence kill me with the shock if they made me go in the sauna contraption again.

'Is there nothing you can give her apart from the steam treatment?' Dad asked, having explained why we'd not been back earlier, saying I'd been bedridden and had only just recovered sufficiently to travel.

'We will now have to start all over again,' the doctor huffed. 'Six treatments, I said. Ideally, it should be weekly. I was being generous saying fortnightly, but you've come back eight weeks later. You're not helping her, you know. You have to stay firm and not let your emotions cloud your judgment.'

I glared at Dad, willing him to say no with all of my heart and soul.

'Are you sure there's no option other than the steam treatment?'

Dr P looked down at us from over the top of his glasses and pushed a file towards Dad, who flipped it open to see before and after photos of all of his patients. They all looked cured in the 'after' photos, with happy smiles and smooth skin.

'No, there's certainly no other treatment,' Dr P continued, 'and if your daughter is strong and brave,' he added, pointing a finger at me, 'I give you a 100 per cent guarantee that she'll be cured, just like these patients here.'

I would have tried *anything* else, but not the torture cabinet again. Anything but that. *Please, Dad...*

My father stood up. 'Well, that's a pity. But I can't see her suffer like I did before. We'll have to find someone else. What do I owe you for today?'

Dad began to write out a cheque and Dr P began to shout. In fact, he didn't stop bellowing until we reached the car.

'You'll regret this! You know you're going to regret this! This is her *only* chance!'

When Dad didn't look back at him, Dr P tried another way.

'You'll be back soon, I promise. Come back to me and I'll only charge you half next time....'

Back in the car, I didn't have to ask Dad what he was thinking: *another bastard quack.* Despite the pain, emotionally I was full of joy and relief for the whole journey home.

When we got back to the house, Anju and Shankerdas thought I'd been cured when they saw me step out of the car with a huge smile on my face. Even better – no one needed to carry me inside screaming.

'I didn't have it!' I said, still unable to believe my luck.

It worked, I thought. *It really did work. Dad heard my silent pleas and refused treatment.*

Telepathy might have worked for me, but nothing else worked to ease my condition. Dad prayed every day that I'd be healed. My skin constantly felt like it was on fire and the only way he could hug me was to gently ease me in against his side by putting his hand on my waist. I often heard him begging forgiveness from God. He'd ask, 'God, give me Bharti's illness,' or 'God, please heal her.' I wondered why he'd wish my condition on himself and I failed to understand how he was suffering, too. As far as I was concerned, I was the one in constant burning pain at the slightest touch, not him.

Looking back now, I see that it was guilt that he felt. I came to understand that the beating he'd given me for talking to the gardener – that senseless, painful beating – was something he regretted every day of his life. And the onset of my illness in the months afterwards was enough to convince him he'd caused it.

Sadly, many children were beaten in those days, yet I was the only child walking around with an incurable skin disease. But Dad couldn't see that. He became a man possessed, having decided he was to blame for the blisters and sores that covered me from top to toe.

Every morning became an interminable agony for me, when my bedsheets were soaked in warm water and gently pried off. As you already know, at times my skin would peel off with the sheets, new blisters bubbling over those ever-present sores. My skin was so fragile that the slightest friction caused the skin to peel off or a blister to appear. Blisters were forever forming, bursting, burning and weeping, as if by some dark magic. Don't get me wrong – it wasn't a permanent agony. The worst ones were those on the palms of my hands, the soles of my feet and my scalp, where the skin was thicker. It was these that actually hurt when they formed. But the rest formed quietly – a silent presence – the pain only present when incised, or when they popped and the fluid came out.

~

CHAPTER 4

Witch Doctors and Priests

W e'd heard it all before: 'I swear he's going to cure your daughter. He's the one!'

It was getter darker. Trees blocked out the sky as we got deeper into the jungle. There was just a faint light penetrating through the treetops – not enough to see by, but there nonetheless. The lights on the car were on full beam as we bumped up and down, every jolt a shot of pain through my weeping sores and blisters.

I looked for the reflection of animal eyes, wondering if they were watching as we jolted and crashed along on the rough, uneven ground, trying to distract myself. Lions, leopards and snakes... I felt like they'd attack us at any moment, just knowing it would be bad if we broke down, instead hoping, praying, that the car would keep going. It was much worse than a safari. A thud made me think a wildcat or snake had landed on top of us, but then I realized it was just branches hitting the roof of the car.

My level of pain was such that we'd been in the car for what felt like hours but was in reality just minutes – it certainly seemed like forever. My skin was in agony. I thought about the witch doctor we had yet to meet on this latest excursion, about the cartoon character I'd seen in books of him with wild hair wearing a lion skin and a bone necklace.

Dad seemed determined to get there quickly. He appeared to know some of the way, which totally amazed me, given this was a jungle he'd never been to before. Every now and then, we'd stop to ask a solitary person where to go next. They'd point and we'd continue on our way, the gears of the Ford Cortina crunching as we made our way through the undergrowth. The wheels bounced off the rocks on the narrow track, making the blisters on my thighs and legs break open and weep. I could feel my skin peeling off as I was jolted from side to side. When Dad wound down the window to ask for yet further directions, my pain ceased for a moment, the musty smell of damp earth creeping in, briefly refocusing my attention.

Eventually, we arrived at a clearing, where before us was the witch doctor's house. It stood in a big patch of light, surrounded by the dark green forest. I'd expected a hut, like in my picture book, but this was a smart brown brick building, just like our house and the missionaries' places. It didn't seem real, out here in the jungle. Chickens pecked beside the house and as we approached the concrete forecourt, the children playing outside scattered and dispersed. I wanted someone to play with while my dad and the witch doctor talked and I hoped the children would come back, but they didn't. *Had I imagined them?* Even the chickens had vanished, leaving just one left pecking at the ground.

A giant of a man strode from the house in a smart grey striped suit and shiny black shoes. Aside from the tiniest piece of bone in his nose, he didn't look at all like the cartoon witch doctors I'd imagined. Those pictures were scary and uncomfortable – but then they'd made me excited and curious, too. This looming man looked too ordinary to be a witch doctor. *Maybe he had another job*, I thought. He might have looked like all the hospital doctors we'd seen, but I was soon to find out just how different his methods were.

Dad greeted him and the witch doctor replied in perfect English. I thought he'd speak Swahili, making gestures to explain what was going to happen, so this came as a surprise. Dad told me to stand to one side until the witch doctor called me, but I wouldn't have said a word anyway, unable to take in what I was seeing: a man in a pinstripe suit standing by a brick house in the middle of the jungle.... And *he* was going to cure me!

As my father and the witch doctor talked, I felt a shiver. There was nowhere to sit down on the veranda, so we had to stand. I remember thinking, *out here, we're prey for wild animals. The jungle can see us.* I was terrified that a creature might come into the clearing and attack. But the men didn't seem scared and I felt better when I realized that Dad had left his gun in the boot of the car. If he hadn't brought it to the house to protect us, then it wasn't needed. Dad was a hunter and he knew when he did or didn't need to carry a gun. *Maybe this wasn't such a bad jungle, after all, and there weren't many wild animals.*

The witch doctor beckoned me to stand before him and Dad showed him my blisters. Although they were obvious for all to see, Dad persisted, continuing to show the witch doctor the blisters and sores on my limbs, demonstrating what he meant. The witch doctor placed his forehead against mine and murmured something I didn't understand. Then he took a stick, drew a circle in the dirt around me and started following the line he'd drawn as he walked along it, all the time chanting a prayer.

'There's an evil spirit inside you,' he began. 'And the only way it can be killed or removed is to drink the water I give you.'

Water is fine, I think. *I can cope with that.* Inside, I'm sighing with relief.

He gestured towards the house for a glass of water and a lady appeared. He took the glass from her without a word, prayed over it and then spat in it. But it wasn't just saliva, which would have been horrible enough. Instead, he'd actually spat phlegm into the glass of water – properly clearing both his throat and the depths of his chest. It was the biggest globule I'd ever seen, and he'd saved it just for me.

I couldn't take my eyes off that glass and the sight of the floating brownish phlegm. *He's mad!* I thought. But then I thought: *What if he can read my mind?* So I began chanting 'Oh dear' over and over in my mind to mask what I was really thinking. I sent what I thought was a telepathic message to Dad, *I'm not drinking that.* But apparently, I actually said it out loud.

Dad looked worried, knowing I was going to refuse to drink it and disobey orders. But the witch doctor was insistent – this would cure me.

He brought the glass towards me and the retching began. But I didn't care that the witch doctor might punish me for challenging him. I would not, could not, drink it.

'I'd rather die than drink this,' I blurted.

To this day, I don't know where I summoned the courage to say that, especially to a witch doctor, but an inner voice gave me that strength. That voice in my head kept screaming, 'Don't drink it. Whatever you do, don't drink it!'

Afraid the witch doctor was going to hit me, I dashed to the car and locked myself in. Dad opened the car doors with his keys and ordered me to come out.

'I'd rather die! I'm sick of all these treatments, I don't want them I don't want to live. Just get that gun out of the boot and shoot me here,' I raged, punching my chest and hoping that was where my heart was situated, intending to do damage. 'Shoot me right now if I'm such a burden to you. I don't care any more. I'm never going to drink that water. You drink it for me, if you must, but don't expect me to.'

I stopped, amazed at my outburst. This was the second time my frustration had caused me to speak rudely to an adult. Yes, I was sick of the treatments, but I didn't mean the rest. Of course I didn't want to die. But I had to show my anger and despair at being dragged to all these inevitably useless, painful and humiliating treatments, so Dad would understand I didn't want to go through this any more. I needed him to appreciate my desperation for my voice to be important, too. I needed to be heard and given a choice about treatments. I guess I was crying out for my worth to be heard.

'I won't force you,' my father said quietly with a look of defeat. 'But at least come and say sorry to him and say thank you. If you don't, he could put a spell on us – and I could do without more curses being put upon us.'

I got out of the car and bowed to the witch doctor, touching his shoe as a mark of respect to an elder.

'I'm sorry, sir, but I cannot drink it. I'm truly very sorry and I don't mean to offend you, sir.'

He turned to my father. 'You do realize it's the malevolent spirit inside her that's refusing. It knows the power of this drink. It's not your daughter saying this.' He threw the contents of the glass away. 'It's lost its power now. It must be swallowed whole to work.'

I looked at the globule of mucus on the ground.

'I can make another one,' he offered, smiling.

Dad started to waver. 'Maybe not so much phlegm next time,' he suggested.

I couldn't believe it. *How could he be so weak? And now it was all going to begin again. How could Dad betray me? Why wasn't he sticking up for me?*

This time, the amount of phlegm produced was smaller. But as far as I was concerned, it still wasn't going to be ingested into my body, no matter how healing it was supposed to be.

Dad took the glass from the witch doctor. 'I'll give it to her this time,' he said. 'She'll drink it if it's from me.'

'No,' the witch doctor said. 'She will drink it from me or not at all.'

But I won't. I won't, Daddyji.

I set my mouth shut and pursed my lips tight as the witch doctor grabbed the glass and put it to my mouth. I looked sideways for a break in the trees so I could run deep into the jungle. *At least if I was eaten by a wild animal, it would be a quick death*, I reasoned.

'It'll be quick,' Dad whispered encouragingly. 'Just close your eyes and take a gulp. It'll be over before you know it.'

I nodded. There was no way out of this.

I looked at the water with its vile ball of mucus. Once again, my inner voice begged me not to drink it. I looked at Dad and suddenly felt sorry for him. We'd come right into the jungle for this. He was driving hundreds of miles and spending thousands of shillings in his quest for a cure just for me – it was hardly for his benefit. Weekends were for resting, but taking me to these places gave him no rest. *If he could do that for me, was it really going to hurt to drink someone's phlegm?* Trying not to look at the slimy globule, I took the tiniest sip.

Just one sip was enough.

I flung the glass to the side and vomited over the witch doctor's shiny shoes and pinstripe trousers. I started to heave again and ran to the car, wiping my mouth on the sleeves of my dress as I went. For the first time, I was grateful I had my skin condition. If I'd been well, I would have been beaten for sure – and not just by Dad, but by the witch doctor, too. Then again, this situation would never have arisen if I *had* been well. I felt resentful towards everyone, especially God, at that point. I remember feeling helpless, doubting God's existence. After all, why would He put a child through all this? The missionaries had said that Jesus had asked all the children who were suffering to come to Him and all their pain and hurt would be taken away. I wondered why He didn't see fit to take *my* pain and suffering away....

The witch doctor strode over the concrete forecourt towards me in his big shoes. He came right up to the car, shaking his finger at me and jabbing it in my direction. His mouth was moving and I knew he was angry. I couldn't hear what he was saying, so I wound the window down a touch. But before he could say more, my father stepped in.

'It's my fault! I should have prepared her,' he said, waving his arms around. 'Sorry! I'm sorry!' he kept repeating, and I shrank back in my seat.

'We'll be back, I promise. Only next time I'll give you double or three times what you're charging to make up for my daughter's rudeness, and to thank you for your patience.'

The witch doctor stopped.

'I will take treble,' he said. 'I have to pay for my trousers and shoes to be cleaned.'

My father gave him a huge wad of notes. 'We'll be back,' he assured.

The witch doctor smiled. 'Next time she'll drink it, I'm sure. It's all new to her and it came as a shock. She'll be prepared next time.'

'Of course, yes. Deepest apologies, sir,' Dad muttered.

'I'm sure you'll be back,' the witch doctor replied, shaking Dad's hand. 'In fact,' he said, his voice dropping, 'I'll pray for your return.'

Was he casting a spell on my father when he said that? I wondered.

We drove off and I didn't look back. As the car sped on, neither Dad nor I said a word. I had a feeling it was over, but just in case he had any doubts, I made my thoughts loud and clear.

'Just in case you were wondering, I'm never going back. Never!'

My father looked straight ahead and carried on driving. There was nothing to indicate he'd heard me.

When we arrived home, my family were waiting to hear all about the witch doctor. Dad tersely told them he needed to rest and went to his room, leaving me to tell everyone what had happened. They were so wide-eyed with horror at the story that their expressions made me laugh out loud. As children we were allowed to laugh freely and I *needed* to laugh. I *needed* the sense of release. That day I'd argued, cried, screamed, retched and vomited – some would say I'd been belligerent – but at least I hadn't swallowed the witch doctor's phlegm. And I'd learned about the jungle. The menace that day was the witch doctor in the smart suit in the brown brick house – and he was meant to be the one helping me. The wild animals I'd imagined goring me were never the real threat.

After so many failed treatments, I understood how far Dad was willing to go to find a cure for me. He was prepared to try anything and I now knew the lengths he'd go to. But I felt like I'd failed him, just as the so-called healings had failed me. And my parents were under siege, in a way, in that they weren't free to socialize at weekends. They were constantly taking me to various healers, priests and gurus in their quest for a cure, meaning they, too, were trapped by my illness. All the fun things we used to do at weekends, like going on safari camping trips and visiting friends, were put on hold in the search for a remedy. Not that they once complained.

Dad treated my blisters at his garage, his place of work. Whenever I was worried about a new blister, I'd go straight to the garage for help. He'd drop everything if a blister needed lancing, even if there was a customer waiting. Customers coming in to get their cars fixed would see him tend my wounds – the first aid box would come out and he'd dress the sores deftly but gently. These customers were usually English, Asian and African, and they came from near and far, so Dad had a constant flow of suggestions and recommendations that I see various doctors all over the world. From the locals shopping at the market next to the bus stop, which was opposite the garage, to those visiting from outside Kabale, everyone knew Dad and was keen to offer advice and ideas. As I had such a visible illness, no one held back when it came to commenting on my condition as they endorsed healers they knew personally or who had cured relatives or friends.

At the Hindu temple in Kabale, other worshippers would advise Mum and Dad about this priest or that psychic or healer or other, claiming that they'd cured their baby's illness or whatever it was. They were so sure that whoever it was would also be able to cure their daughter – me. Whenever a new priest came to town, people would flock to him and word got around.

Initially, Dad ignored these suggestions, but over time he came to be more open. He believed there were some things in life that couldn't be explained but that there was a cure out there somewhere – we just didn't know what it was yet. I sensed that he wouldn't forgive himself if we missed out on a cure just because he personally didn't believe in it. I remember him once even declaring, 'Whatever religion cures you, I will follow it.'

Not only were there these well-wishers, but also the doctors. And as you know, some refused to see me, others made me drink strange bitter concoctions, and still more tortured me in things like steam cabinets. No wonder we became disillusioned. To this day, Anju has a phobia of portable steam cabinets. Her husband, who is interested in Ayurveda (a Hindu system of medicine based on the idea of balance in bodily systems that uses diet, herbal treatment and yogic breathing), wanted to buy one, but she refused to let him bring one of those contraptions into the house, not after seeing what I went through.

And then there was Mum, a great believer in spiritual healing. She often said to Dad that he shouldn't just dismiss things on a whim, urging him to at least try. They were both desperate to make me well. And I understand, too, how several sets of beliefs can co-exist. My father was an educated man – a business owner, philanthropist and a believer in equality for women when it came to education and career paths. Despite all the values and beliefs he held about how women should act, he went against the norm and even educated his daughters when many families frowned on giving girls any education at all, given we were destined to become wives and mothers. Yet, he lived in a country with a deep belief in black magic – a country in which no one wanted to offend a witch doctor and risk being cursed. Still, he would have been prepared to try anything, and put aside any doubts or prejudices in the hope that this next treatment might work, even if it meant engaging in things outside the norm.

Curses and witchcraft were the given explanation for so many ills in Uganda – from businesses failing to sickness, and from childlessness to death. In Uganda, you couldn't pretend that the belief in magic didn't exist. It was soaked into the fabric of our lives. To survive in society, you needed to both fear and respect it.

Dad tried to take a stand against superstition by promoting education. Many Africans came to work in Dad's garage who at that time were disadvantaged. Dad often paid for them to go away for training and he'd also ask his employees if they had a son or daughter who needed educating, even agreeing to pay for them, as well. He believed that if one person in a family was educated, they may be able to help the rest of the family, thereby becoming self-sufficient.

He paid for one bright young man to go to boarding school and supported the boy's family while he was away. The boy finished his education, got married and found a good job. Then this young man decided for whatever reason that his mother-in-law was a witch and was practising witchcraft on him and his family. So he took a can of fuel to set her alight. While trying to burn her, he splashed fuel on himself, caught fire and died.

Dad was so angry and disappointed. 'I wanted him to make a better life for himself,' I heard him telling Mum. 'But with this stupid belief that his mother-in-law was a witch, he's wasted it all.'

After the disaster with the witch doctor, Dad seemed to accept defeat in his quest to find a cure for me, instead passing the baton of finding a healer to Mum. After all, it was her faith that had guided her to find me, an abandoned baby, in hospital on Ward 21. If a woman who was seven months' pregnant knew that I must be part of the family and had followed her dream to adopt me, he believed that surely she was therefore the one to find the cure.

Mum was very spiritual, but she was superstitious, too. We were told not to take food from strangers or to visit any house without our parents knowing our whereabouts. 'Black magic can be done,' my mother would say, 'so don't touch or eat anything that's left lying around. No sweets or food.' It was deemed fine to eat fruit straight from the tree – as I had done, stealing the guavas – but even fallen fruit was forbidden. This wasn't a rule just for us. In my family, all of our relatives and friends brought their children up the same way. In Western culture, the equivalent would be telling children not to talk to or take sweets from strangers. In Uganda, there was a very real fear that children could become victims of black magic.

Every Saturday, Anju and I would go to our friend's house to play. We had our own route, which began with a scramble through the hedge at the back of our house, then to the gully. Over the narrow stream of water was an equally narrow bridge that took us to our friend's. One such Saturday when I was younger, on our way back home we saw something that didn't look right. On the bridge, blocking our path, was an offering – a circle of purple, yellow and red flowers with some white candles in the centre that had been lit.

'That's weird!' I said.

I stopped in my tracks, looking at the way the flowers had been so carefully arranged.

'Don't touch it! It's black magic!' Anju cautioned.

Trembling, Anju refused to cross the small bridge as I scoffed at her not to be so silly. I didn't believe in black magic at all, so I kicked my way through it, scattering the flowers and candles across the bridge.

When we got home, we immediately told Mum what we'd seen. She paled and ran from the house, but when we reached the bridge, there was nothing there. Everything had disappeared – not a petal nor a candle in sight either on the bridge, in the water or on either side of the bridge. Frantically, Mum searched everywhere. I peered into the gully and, to my surprise, I couldn't see so much as one petal anywhere, either. Her reaction was one of panic, suggesting to me that the offering I'd destroyed had had some greater significance. Hands on hips, I told her exactly where the flowers were.

'But there are no petals here, nothing.' She was distraught. 'Black magic is at work here. You should never have walked through it. Someone's cursed it. They intended that you walked into it, and you did just that.'

She prayed that day with me at her side, asking the goddess Mataji to protect me.

When the blisters first came, Mum was convinced someone had caused them with black magic. She often reproached me, telling me I should never have kicked the flowers and petals all those years ago. She kept asking me why I'd been so foolish. But then at other times she'd muse that I was just a child and that I wasn't to know. Mum decided that prayer was the answer to the curse that had caused the blisters, so began trips to Hindu priests for special healing ceremonies and to join them in prayer to remove the curse.

These priests might give me things to take like a tea made with ground leaves, which tasted really bitter, or they'd ask me to sit in a circle of limes. I'd have to remain really still, which was difficult when the pressure on my skin was so painful. Then the limes were sliced in two. If they were black inside, the evil had been taken out of my body and into the limes, meaning the prayers had worked.

Or I'd be given a coconut to hold for a very long time while the priests said prayers and threw chillies into the ritual fire. I'd take the coconut home and place it under my bed then return to the temple a day or a week later. (According to Mum, the frequency depended on how poor the priest was.) The coconut would be broken and, once again, if it was black inside, it meant that the evil spirit was out of me.

And so the priests chanted and poured holy water over me, sprinkling holy ash onto my forehead. *This* was going to cure me. My parents were also asked to place a garland of chillies over the entrances to our home to ward off any further evil spirits, which they duly did.

Each ritual usually took about half an hour to an hour, depending on an individual priest's belief as to how deep my problem was. The deeper they thought it was, the longer the ritual took.

Although some of my blistering was less intense, it continued as before. My skin remained fragile and sensitive to the touch. I was far from cured and I felt guilty for not feeling better. Each time, the priest would ask, 'Do you feel better now, do you feel lighter?' I felt compelled to say, 'Yes, definitely,' but it didn't really matter what I really felt inside, because I didn't dare insult the priest. As a child, I knew about respect, so I'd say, 'Yes, I feel a lot better, thank you.'

And my mum would ask me in the car, '*Do* you feel better?'

And I'd say, 'Yes, much better, thank you!'

Not only did I want it to work, but she did, too. Only the next day, a blister would suddenly appear and soon there would be more.

Then came the recriminations. My mother was told the healing hadn't worked because I didn't have my eyes closed when the prayers were spoken. Another priest simply said that I shouldn't have got myself into such a precarious situation in the first place and that my mother was to blame – she should have warned me not to touch or go near the flowers and candles that I'd kicked over; I'd been deliberately targeted.

A further explanation for the lack of a cure was my adoption – I didn't have my mother's blood. Or they'd say things like, 'It's because she doesn't have faith. If she truly believed, she'd be cured by now.'

But I'd prayed every night to all the gods I could think of, including the Christian one, saying 'I believe, I believe.'

Then I decided that believing only in Jesus would cure me, so I renounced every other god. In the morning, I'd wake up expectantly like the leper in the Bible, expecting to see my skin all smooth, strong and blister-free, but it never happened. I wondered how I could convince Jesus I believed in Him, because nothing I said or did was enough. In despair, I eventually came to the conclusion that maybe God just didn't like me enough to want to cure me.

Each of these doctors, gurus, witch doctors and specialists all expected, and received, a hefty donation. The bigger the donation, the more powerful the prayer. One guru told my mother, 'The curse is too powerful. This will take months of prayers.'

Thankfully, not all doctors or priests we talked to were out to make money. Some said they'd never seen a skin disease like mine and couldn't offer a cure or an explanation. They refused to accept money and offered prayers or gave the names of doctors who might be able to help. Even at nine years old, I remembered their kindness and gentle words.

One priest explained my illness as kismet or fate. 'This is something she has to go through. The teaching is that maybe she made somebody suffer, maybe she rejected someone with a skin condition, in a past life.' Their belief was that my skin condition was a way of making my soul understand my actions. 'There's nothing you can do to change this girl's destiny,' he continued. 'This isn't a curse – this is from God. She must go through this.'

My favourite priest was the last we were to visit. We'd heard about a very famous priest and psychic who was touring the world and was coming to a town near us in Uganda. These priests didn't have names – they were sometimes called *panditji* (the 'ji' is a title of respect) and they, like many others I saw, came from the Hindu tradition. If this *panditji* had had another name, I would have remembered it, because his remedy was to be the best ever.

Mum was desperate for us to go and see him. Maybe *he* would tell us if I could be cured and, if so, when. The *panditji*'s words, however, weren't quite what my parents had hoped for.

When Mum gently pushed me forwards to stand before him, the *panditji* said I had a curse put on me by someone who wanted to claim me but couldn't have me. The curse was that I'd die young and my family would suffer by my absence. I wouldn't live to be a teenager.

Later, I realized that Mum must have believed this, because it chimed with the story about my birth father turning up for my adoption hearing, then demanding money when he couldn't have me just to grant the adoption. So my disease was supposedly a lesson from my birth father – he'd cursed me with an incurable condition so I'd suffer, and then my parents would suffer for two reasons: first in watching me suffer and then in witnessing my death.

The *panditji* told Mum he could say prayers to prevent my early death, but he couldn't completely remove the curse because it was too powerful. As there were no guarantees that I'd live longer, he said, 'Give her whatever she wants. Nothing should be refused.' Sweets (I loved this priest); ice cream (my love was bigger); chocolates (I wanted to worship him); and finally, to complete my adoration: 'Don't scold her, don't chastise her. You may not have too long with her, so make sure she's completely happy in your care from now on.'

I didn't really take in the bit about the early death. And being a teenager seemed so far into the future, anyway. I was just ecstatic that I could have all the sweets I wanted in the world, whenever I wanted them.

When we returned home, my excitement was short-lived. 'What a load of rubbish,' my father scowled, and that was that. He was angry that the *panditji* had dared to say my life would soon end, so he didn't want to hear any more after that. No more priests, *swamijis*, imams, pastors or gurus; no more famous *panditjis*, no more witch doctors. I did wonder how a man who thought a globule of witch doctor phlegm could cure another person could be so against a priest whom I thought very wise – not only that, but also the best one we'd met, given he'd wanted me to have everything I asked for.

To my surprise, I realized I was being given first choice of all the treats he and Mum bought from time to time; but they were careful to share them with my siblings, too.

My telling of the so-called prominent specialist doctors of Uganda, and of the witch doctor and priests, has at times been met with disbelief, as if it's unbelievable that a parent's love for a sick child could make them lose all sense of reason. These people found it incredible that desperation, that an endless quest for a cure, could lead a parent and child into unique – and at times abusive – situations. Either that, or they simply didn't believe that Dr P, with his torture cabinet, actually existed. Or that Dr H pinched me, never mind that my father hit him.

These responses undermine a child's need to be heard. Not only that, but it's also about an adult's need for validation. I'm so grateful when I receive validation for my story, even today – as, when I look back, even I find it hard to accept that those extraordinary things happened to me. What I take from those experiences now is how much my parents valued me. It was their unwavering intention to find a cure that gave me such a sense of worth as a child. And I needed that sense of worth, because at school I was continually being bullied because of my skin condition.

Most of my classmates shunned me. They didn't want to be near me, afraid they'd catch my disease. If I sat next to somebody in class, they'd just get up and find another desk. Only Anju sat next to me, or one or two best friends we had, who always accepted me unconditionally. Occasionally, they'd ask if my blisters hurt, but otherwise they never mentioned my condition, for which I was grateful.

I was so conscious of my skin and how it looked that I dreaded the thought of drawing attention to myself in class. Once a month, Matron would dose us all with castor oil mixed with a sweet syrup. In Uganda, children were prone to getting worms and this mixture was popular at the time, as it was believed it cleansed our digestive tracts. The sweet syrup was actually what de-wormed us, whereas the castor oil was meant to make us strong.

Matron would get her spoon – just the one – and we'd stand in line to be given the mixture. Some of the children would whinge and say things like, 'Urgh, I don't want her to have it before me. I might catch what she's got!' Or the more spiteful among them said, 'Don't you dare go in front of me! I don't want to eat your disease.' So I always went last in the queue, to avoid the shame of listening to those words.

One particular day, Matron lined us all up ready for the treatment but stopped me in my tracks.

'Bharti,' she said, 'I want you at the front.'

'Oh no, I'm all right here, miss.'

I panicked, feeling the whole class looking at me in a mixture of horror and absolute disbelief. I was being made to go to the front and they were being made to lick the spoon after me. As nobody wanted to be second in line, a great shuffling and jostling broke out.

'You *will* come to the front, Bharti,' she insisted.

'But I can't.'

'You can and you will.' She turned to the class and challenged them. 'Do any of you have a problem with that?'

'No, miss,' they chorused.

And so I went first.

That really boosted my sense of worth. I was embarrassed at the same time, but somebody respected me. Matron saw my worth through everything – my shyness, my scars, the humiliation and my fear of constant rejection.

After that, no one questioned where I stood in the queue. I still preferred to be last, so as not to draw attention to myself, but for the first time, I felt I had a choice, thanks to Matron.

When I was going through tough times, Anju would try to cheer me up, recalling this very occasion. 'Do you remember when you stood at the front of the line for Matron?'

Matron taught me a valuable lesson about worth: that you don't have to accept the way others treat you. You can fight for yourself when you choose to; and if you have the sense of worth to fight back, others will join you in that fight, too.

I know my parents were following their Divine voices in trying to find a cure for me. The voices that said, 'Never give up on your daughter.' They must have spent thousands of shillings and driven thousands of miles to find that elusive cure for my illness, and they did so unquestioningly. This showed me how much they valued me, raising my sense of worth. And perhaps I value the sacrifices they made today more so than I did then. Not just financially, but it was also their total acceptance, where they gave of their time unconditionally, at the expense of my siblings, who never once complained. I honestly believe that if my parents had been asked to hand everything over to cure me, they'd gladly have done so.

~

CHAPTER 5

My Dream and Idi Amin

At school one day, we were asked to write about a recent dream. The dream I recalled and wrote down in my exercise book is still inscribed on my memory:

> A line of camouflaged army cars and a crowd is gathering in the town below. We're all asking, 'Where have all these visitors come from?' When the cars arrive, we're waving at them. Hawkers are rushing forwards to sell their wares.

> There are soldiers in these cars. At first they're smiling, but then they start shooting. People are screaming and running, and in the chaos I can't find my family. I can't move. People all around me are running and falling, but I'm just standing here.

Then a soldier turns and points his gun at me. I know he's going to shoot me.

At that point, I'd woken up. A sense of relief coursed through me that I was safe and in my bed.

'That's a strange dream, Bharti.'

Our English teacher cast her eyes over my words for a second time. She decided that she wanted to show what I'd written to the headmistress of our school, and a few hours later I was summoned to the head's office, my exercise book lying open on her desk.

'Did you dream this, or did you read about this somewhere?' she asked.

I believed I was in trouble, so I whispered. 'It was a dream – a real one,' I said. 'Miss asked us to write about a dream we'd had, which is what I did.'

'What I think,' the English teacher said after a pause that seemed to go on forever, 'is that you have a very vivid imagination. You must have read about soldiers in a book somewhere.'

I nodded, believing it was disrespectful to contradict an elder, particularly the headmistress. In a way, it was a relief to agree with her. That dream had been troubling me and I wanted to believe it was just my imagination. No one wants to have a gun pointing at them. No one.

As I turned to leave, she said something strange.

'Don't talk of this dream to anyone, Bharti. In fact, I'm going to remove the page it's written on from your book. I want to keep it safe.'

I didn't say anything further or think to question it. In hindsight, knowing Idi Amin had just come into power, I now wonder if perhaps the adults had heard things and she didn't want my dream to be read by anyone, knowing how people might disappear if my words came into the wrong hands. The risks would have been unthinkable, not only for me and my family, but also for the teachers and the school.

'Why did the headmistress want to see you? Were you in trouble?' the children asked when I returned to class.

Having been told not to discuss the dream, I replied, 'She wanted to ask me if I was feeling any better because of these blisters.'

That explanation seemed satisfactory to all.

In 1971, a year after my dream, a military coup saw Idi Amin seize power in Uganda. When our new president visited our small town of Kabale, he came with great pomp and ceremony. All the schools congregated in the little stadium and sang the national anthem.

As school children, we'd sung loudly, to waves of applause. Welcoming our new leader in the stadium that day, we'd all sensed the promise of change – better lives ahead. We sang that anthem with such joy, but none of us knew then just how ironic those lyrics would prove to be as time unfolded under Idi Amin's reign. At the time we were singing about unity, freedom, liberty and togetherness, but this was far from our reality.

In the stadium, I remembered the dream but immersed myself in the celebrations. The soldiers smiled as they danced and laughed, mingling freely with the crowd. They handed out sweets to all of the children and we thought they were very kind as everybody danced with abandonment. Idi Amin was given a rapturous welcome and was greeted with loud cheers when he stood up at the podium – in our eyes, he was a celebrity who would bring about the birth of a new era.

Little did we know then that my dream was a nightmare about to come true.

The rumours began soon after the coup – whispers that people were disappearing, never to be seen again. The adults worried about not feeling safe any more with Idi Amin as leader, and Dad and his friends spent hours talking about the countries they could emigrate to. We heard talk of Canada, India and the USA. Dad even spoke about England, as he still wanted me to see the specialist who had been recommended years before – a Dr Emerson in Berkshire. Both of my parents had British passports, which they'd obtained long before Uganda became independent in 1962. Dad had been given a British passport because he'd served in the British Army in the Second World War, so he figured that England was the country that would welcome us if we needed to leave. We realized that the adults around us didn't feel safe. Everyone looked tense.

If anyone talked publicly about Idi Amin, it was to be in positive terms only. They praised how good he was for Uganda and what a great leader he was. To say anything negative at all could have led to that person disappearing or being killed. I noticed that, at home, if our parents talked about leaving Uganda or about people being killed, they spoke in whispers in the bedroom only.

I remember us becoming very excited at the prospect of leaving and asking when we were going to go to England. We were loud and were scolded roundly. Dad said that if we so much as spoke about it outside the home to anyone, including our friends, he'd kill us before Idi Amin's soldiers did. These types of conversation were to be private, within the four walls of our house only. He trusted us to keep quiet and we understood how dangerous it was to speak of leaving the country.

Dad often went to Kampala, the capital, to order supplies for his garage, and on one such visit he managed to secure passports for all the family except me, because I didn't have a birth certificate and the embassy wouldn't accept my adoption certificate. To get round this, my name was added to my mum's passport.

The brutality of Idi Amin's regime was to become a horrific reality for our family.

'I'm not going hunting any more,' Dad announced quietly to my mum one day. 'It's too dangerous.'

I didn't know what Dad meant then – wasn't hunting always dangerous?

When Shankerdas' friends came over to the house, he began telling us all the story of how, that morning, he and Dad had stumbled upon a mass grave. While out hunting, a foul smell had assaulted their nostrils, and in trying to locate its source they'd happened upon hundreds of corpses piled in a pit – the people who were said to have disappeared, but had clearly been murdered by Idi Amin's men. We listened agog, not realizing Dad had entered the room.

'Don't you dare!' My father got hold of my brother's ears and shook him firmly. 'Don't you *ever* speak of what you saw there. You don't know who could be listening and you'll get us all killed, do you understand?'

As children, we had a naturally macabre fascination to hear more. There were stories of various atrocities and we'd listen wide-eyed with the wonder and horror of it all as Shankerdas and his friends gave a whispered account of what was happening in town. Of people kidnapped by Idi Amin's secret police, imprisoned, tortured and murdered. From what they said, they were just shot in the street right in front of people.

Soldiers went into hospitals, streets and homes killing people who had been part of or sided with President Obote after he'd been deposed by Idi Amin in a coup. Our house servants steadily began to leave our employ, wanting to be with their families during this distressing time. We wept our goodbyes, sensing it was unlikely we'd see them again now we were due to leave Uganda, though we were forbidden from speaking of our intentions.

What Shankerdas didn't tell me about was the warning Dad and he had been given during one of their trips. They'd been hunting in Queen Elizabeth National Park not far from Mbarara, a garrison town in the Ankole region. From a hillside, they'd seen a convoy of army vehicles led by the presidential car. My father didn't want to be seen, so he and Shankerdas had hidden behind a thicket until the convoy had passed. Then they'd gone down the hill into the village, where villagers told them not to return because it was too dangerous.

By all accounts, trucks loaded with corpses had been seen going through the village every day. Villagers had noticed that, on one truck, two of the bodies were white males. The villagers remembered the convoy with the two white men because they'd never seen a dead white person before.

The following day, on the front page of the *Uganda Argus* newspaper, there were reports that both an American journalist and an American academic had been killed. President Amin denied having anything to do with the deaths. Shankerdas ran to my father, shouting that the white people seen by the villagers could have been the missing Americans. My father scolded him severely. He said no one must know they'd been in that region, or what they'd heard, as it could put our family at risk and we could all be killed because of what we knew. He didn't want news to spread that we all knew of the killings before the newspaper had even reported it, and especially not that they'd seen President Amin's car in that area at that time, too.

The sense of fear in our town was palpable and began to infect us all. Soldiers were everywhere and it was deemed too dangerous to leave the house to visit friends or go shopping. We lived in fear of being stopped, interrogated or, worse, never being seen again – the reality of living in Uganda at the time. We'd listen to Dad's friends reeling off names of people who had disappeared or been shot dead – far too many to list here.

Kabale was near the borders of Rwanda and the Congo and, to prove you weren't a spy from either country, a new rule was introduced whereby you had to carry an ID card. If you didn't produce it on demand, you could be shot, no questions asked. Shankerdas and his friend once sneaked out to go into town and got stopped by a soldier, who demanded to see their ID. Shankerdas, however, had left his at home. The soldier then asked Shankerdas who his father was and he replied, 'Mr Chand, the garage owner at Dhir Engineering.'

The soldier told him that as Dad had fixed and serviced all of their cars, including Idi Amin's, he was considered a friend and he therefore he wouldn't shoot his friend's son on this occasion. My sisters and I realized he'd been very lucky, because some soldiers didn't even stop to ask names or give people a chance to provide an explanation. Shankerdas didn't dare tell of this encounter, as he was fairly certain that he'd be soundly beaten, having been warned never to leave the house without his ID.

One day, a knock at the front door summoned one of the servants. On our veranda stood President Amin himself, accompanied by guards. We were told to go to our bedrooms and not come out under any circumstances. For some reason, Dad didn't want him to see us. At the time, none of us knew why the President had turned up on our doorstep, or why Dad wanted to keep us hidden.

The truth was that girls were being abducted by soldiers and Dad needed to protect us from being seen. At the time, we'd felt frustrated that someone so important had come to visit and we'd not been allowed to meet him. But when we discovered what he already knew, we remained forever grateful that Dad had spared us from an introduction.

It turned out that President Amin had a request: he wanted Dad to shoot animals for him and his soldiers. (There was a culture of big-game hunting with Idi Amin and his men. A former poacher and smuggler, the President encouraged poaching and hunting when he came to power.) He'd heard that Dad was a renowned hunter and for Dad to refuse would have been folly. My father reluctantly agreed and subsequently killed antelope, warthogs and other animals on command within the national parks closest to Kabale –

Bwindi Impenetrable National Park and the Kigezi Game Reserve, on the border of Uganda and the Congo. Dad accompanied Idi Amin and his men on these trips monthly.

We were blissfully ignorant of just how trapped Dad had become. Having seen the horrific sight of that mass grave in the jungle and the growing tension on the street, it felt wrong for him to shoot animals that weren't usually killed for food. The President's regime was one of cruelty not only for the people; he also had a penchant for creatures Dad would never have hunted: giraffes, crocodiles, zebras – anything that moved was on Idi Amin's menu. He even forced my father to shoot elephants for their meat, and on one occasion Idi Amin kept four of the feet to turn into stools, one of which he gave to my father as a gift.

Even more distressing for my father was Idi Amin's command that he shoot a pregnant leopard. My father had never shot a pregnant animal and he was mortified the day he killed her. He was also ordered to kill eland and greater kudu, a type of antelope that resembles cows. As Hindu-Sikhs, we never ate beef, as in Hinduism cows are considered sacred. When Dad was forced to shoot these animals, he took baths to cleanse himself and prayed for forgiveness that he'd committed such a sin. Idi Amin's thirst for blood, both animal and human, seemed unquenchable. We heard wild talk that he and his soldiers threw people to the crocodiles and that he kept the severed heads of human beings at his palace. It was said, too, that Idi Amin ate his enemies – a butcher rumoured to feed on the flesh of human beings.

'He's forcing me to commit great sins,' Dad had despaired. 'He doesn't understand that when I hunt, I kill only animals that are traditionally eaten, and I share the meat with everyone. But killing pregnant animals for the sake of sport!' he'd complain in a low voice to Mum at the dinner table. 'God will never forgive me.' (I think killing pregnant animals resonated emotionally for Dad because of the number of children my mum had lost through miscarriages and in stillbirth in the past.)

'It's okay,' Mum would soothe. 'I think God will understand that you have no choice.'

I know that the teachers at our missionary school shared my father's sense of restriction. The teachers had to keep secret the fact that several of Idi Amin's children were pupils. I later heard how the staff couldn't say anything negative about the President's regime or even mention it, because they didn't know if the children would recount it to their fathers. It was a very stressful period at the school and the lives of some staff members were devastated by Idi Amin's regime. By the end of this military dictator's rule in 1979, it's believed that thousands had been executed and slaughtered – massacred in their droves. The absolute discretion around the identity of Idi Amin's children at the school was designed to protect not only his children, but also the lives of other children and the staff. One teacher told me that the children themselves were lovely – thankfully, they didn't have their father's traits.

Then came the day when we saw the very same soldiers that I'd seen in my dream. Days earlier, they'd confiscated every car in Kabale, and this particular day we saw the soldiers driving the vehicles they'd stolen in a slow convoy down the hill. Some residents rushed into town in the hope they'd get their cars back, but others sensed the danger. Shopkeepers hurriedly shut their doors and barricaded themselves inside.

As soon as the soldiers had entered the main street in town, they'd started shooting at random. Men, women and children turned and ran for their lives. We heard later that many people died that day. It didn't matter to them who you were – anyone was fair game.

I also saw my dad stricken with grief. He had sent one of the workers from his garage to town on an errand, and news came through that he'd died. Dad felt responsible and was consumed with reproach and self-blame. He questioned himself repeatedly, wishing he hadn't sent him, wishing he'd known what would happen that day.

Knowing the main breadwinner had died, Dad went to see the worker's family to pay for the funeral and to give them a large amount of money – not that it was any recompense. He enrolled the man's children in a school and paid up front for their education into adulthood. Dad's wish was that they'd make something of themselves and his belief was that if they were educated or pursued a skill, they'd be able to provide for their families in the future.

I pondered long and hard about the senseless murder of that man. When someone we know dies, we spend so much time wondering if we could have done something to prevent their death. Yet, how can we protect them when faced with someone corrupted by the power of a gun? I began to realize that when some people hold a gun, they become poisoned by an evil that turns their hearts to stone and eats into the core of their humanity. Evil blinds them so they can't see the worth of any living being, so consumed are they with the desire to kill. For some it was a choice to kill another, while others felt compelled to commit such atrocities in order to prove their worth and allegiance to Idi Amin.

As children at that time, we heard many horror stories of soldiers going into hospitals, murdering newborn babies before raping and killing women who had just given birth. Newborn babies were killed in the maternity ward on the pretext of being spies just because they didn't have ID cards. The same justification was used for hacking their mothers to death where they lay in their hospital beds.

Talk of going to England became more urgent between my mother and father, yet there were times when they were reluctant to leave. They questioned whether they should wait and see if Idi Amin would be overthrown in a coup, just like when he'd come to power. They wondered who they could trust to look after the house and business in their absence, which Dad had built from scratch. Leaving Uganda was never meant to be permanent. His plan was to leave us in England while I got my treatment and then we'd join him a couple of years or so later once Uganda was safe again. His belief was that surely a dictator like Idi Amin wouldn't last long.

It's rumoured that Idi Amin had set his mind on marrying the daughter of an Asian millionaire. He was duped into thinking the girl's father had agreed to the match and the family used this time to flee Uganda in their private jet. Naturally furious, in August 1972 Idi Amin gave the order that all Asians had to leave Uganda within 90 days, by 8 November of that year. The deadline was then reduced to just 45 days. He said that if any Asian chose to stay, they had to accept Ugandan citizenship and be prepared to marry Africans, or be taken to a military concentration camp. Those who refused to comply were subjected to violence and intimidation.

Dad never got to see England or Dr Emerson. He died just a year before we left Uganda.

CHAPTER 6

Losing Dad

A few months after those discussions about leaving Uganda, Dad had become ill. He'd been forced by Adi Amin to go on another hunting trip and when he returned home on one particular occasion, he looked pale and exhausted. He was told to rest, but Dad being Dad, he kept working. He'd been unwell for some weeks and we'd noticed that his skin colour and the whites of his eyes were taking on a yellow tinge. A visit by our family GP, Dr Desai, confirmed that Dad had jaundice, which required specialist treatment that could only be provided in Mulago Hospital. But still he kept working.

When Dad's best friend came to see him, Dad had no recollection of the visit, looking puzzled when Mum mentioned his visit.

'Don't you remember?' she asked. 'He was just here....'

After that conversation, we later discovered that Dad instructed his nephew, Pritam Paaji ('paaji' means brother, a term we use to refer to older brothers) to take over the garage. He'd put his affairs in order and had gone to say goodbye to each of the young men whose education he was paying for – and, if needed, to offer more money for them to finish their studies. My father knew he wouldn't be around to see either his proteges or our family business thrive. As children, we had no idea of the severity of the situation, blissfully unaware of the dark days ahead.

As his health declined further, Dad took to his bed. Then one day he announced he was going to Mulago Hospital in Kampala.

My father wore the same stoic expression as always and, as he said he was capable of driving himself, we had no idea just how ill he was. We made him promise he'd bring us back presents, which was the routine whenever he went away. It seemed he hugged each of us more tightly before getting into the car. Then he embraced Mum, which came as a shock to us, as they never touched or hugged each other in front of us. This was the Indian cultural way then, and still is in many families, public displays of affection not being considered the norm.

Mum begged to go with him, but Dad insisted she needed to stay to look after the children. No one was to accompany him on what turned out to be his final journey on Earth. We chased the car, waving and calling, but he didn't look back at us. We had no idea that this would be the last time we'd see him alive.

Since Dad had left the family home, my mother had spent most of her time crying and praying. Mum's fervent prayers to Goddess Mataji at our family altar began the moment Dad went away to the hospital.

'My respected and loving Mataji, have pity! Make my husband well.' The chant always ended with, 'Bring him back to us. *Please*, bring him back. I know you have the power.'

Then my mother, as always, had a feeling things weren't right. In the early hours of the morning, a couple of weeks after Dad's departure for hospital, she'd summoned us from our beds and gathered us round the altar in their bedroom. On the altar were framed pictures of the Sikh gurus and those of Hindu deities, including:

Ganeshj – the son of Lord Shiva and Goddess Parvati, the remover of all obstacles and problems

Mataji – the supreme Mother Goddess of all gods, goddesses and humankind

Lakshmi – the goddess of wealth and purity

Lord Shiva – the supreme and most powerful god, both creator and destroyer

Guru Nanak – the founder of the Sikh faith

Offerings of flowers ensured the deities would grant good health, wealth and prosperity, along with fruits to make our hearts become as sweet as our offerings. A *diya* lamp was placed in front of Mataji and we stood there motionless, as instructed by Mum. I was carrying my little brother, Shiv, still warm and sleepy from his bed.

Mum bent over the *diya* and held a match to the wick. Incense was burning to wake the god or goddess, to symbolize that prayers were beginning, and the sweet smell of incense filling the air symbolized that the god was present. The *diya* flickered into life for a second, then the flame blew out. I thought it strange that it wouldn't light, because there was no breeze – the room was perfectly still. My mother took this as a very bad omen.

'Have pity,' she wept. 'Mataji, have pity. Please don't make me a widow.'

Her raw anguish cut through like a saw or an animal gnawing a bone.

'Look, look!' She drew us all closer. 'Five children. I *need* him. If not for me, do it for them. Don't leave them fatherless. Where will we go? What will we do? It's too soon for you to take my children's father. Please,' she implored, 'take my life instead, but bring him back....'

I don't know how long we stood there. My mother was wailing, but there was no obvious reason why she was so distressed. No one had come with any news of our father. No one! Yet, the entreaties went on. Why was she moaning and keening like that at a mere picture of Mataji?

She struck another match above the *diya* then whispered, 'If you've listened to my prayer, Mataji, this *diya* will light.'

She began to repeat herself over and over, using up not one but two boxes of matches, until the altar was strewn with half-blackened sticks. But still the *diya* wouldn't light.

It's only now that I understand how significant the *diya* was to Mum. When someone was very ill, you lit a *diya* and you never allowed the flame to go out. If the flame burned strong, it meant that the person was getting better. If the *diya* went out, it meant that the person had died. So strong was Mum's belief in this ritual that with each futile attempt to light it, she'd let out a cry of frustration and despair.

We remained silent, not understanding Mum's desperation. It was Shankerdas who spoke first.

'I think Daddyji's dead.'

His words stirred a horrible knowing inside me. Mum gazed into space, her eyes empty. There was no life, no light. No more tears, no more weeping. He'd gone. Nothing could be done.

On the day the *diya* didn't light, our phone started ringing, but Mum didn't answer.

It was only when my cousin's wife, Gurmit Jair Kaur, Bhabiji to us (meaning sister-in-law, as we never refer to elders by their names), arrived without warning that we knew something momentous had happened. She rarely visited. As soon as Mum saw her on the veranda, she started wailing. Her arrival was the confirmation we dreaded: our father had died.

More women started arriving, then men. White sheets were laid out on the floor and everyone in the house came and sat on them, as was the custom when somebody died. It's only now that I understand they're a symbol of purity and that the colour white is a mark of respect to both the departed and the family. The women had dressed Mum in the traditional white *salwar* (Indian-style trousers) and *kameeze* with a white *chunni*. It was peculiar seeing her devoid of make-up and not wearing her usual bright colours.

People were asking Mum what had happened. They knew, but it was their attempt to bring her out of her stupor and help her grieve by speaking it out loud, making it real.

It was late afternoon when we heard the sound of a car approaching. We recognized the sound of the engine. My dad's car! A pulse of joy coursed through me and we rushed towards the veranda to greet him. When Pritam Paaji and Sohan Paaji, my dad's nephews, brought him out of the car, I froze in shock. Dad was sleeping on a stretcher, but his face was covered. He was fine, after all. The *diya* had been wrong!

I heard a shriek from my mother and looked up to see a friend catch her fall before she hit the floor of the veranda. All of the adults started wailing and weeping at the sight of him. I'd never seen a dead body before and couldn't believe this was my dad. When Anju started sobbing, I knew then that he'd died. Pritam Paaji had been named as next of kin and had been called by the hospital to say Dad had passed away and would he come and collect him from Mulago Hospital. When the death certificate came later, it confirmed that Dad had died from a brain haemorrhage.

I held my little brother, Shiv, comforting him as he sobbed, not understanding what was happening. But what he was witnessing was frightening for any child. Women were wailing, weeping, thumping their chests and hitting their heads. Mum lay prone on the sofa, semi-conscious.

We were ushered away to Mum and Dad's bedroom, where we'd prayed for Dad's return just hours before. We were told that we mustn't come out of their room until we were called. No breakfast. No lunch. Everyone was consumed with grief that day. One of the servants gave us small bananas to eat in the bedroom. We noticed that they all looked upset and sad, too.

When we heard our mum screaming later, we ran out, despite having been told to stay put – no one stopped us. She was kneeling beside my dad, kissing his face all over, his lips. She kept pleading with him to come back.

'Look. Look at our children.' She took hold of each of us. 'Tell your daddy you're here.'

She got hold of our hands one by one and made us touch his forehead. I was shocked by the feel of him, the icy, freezing-cold sensation of his skin. Why was no one putting a quilt on him to warm him up? Why did he have cotton wool in his nostrils and ears? None of this made sense. It was only later that I came to understand that cotton wool was placed in orifices so bodily fluids didn't leak out.

Someone cooked for us. I thought that the hard lump in my throat that wouldn't let me cry wouldn't let me eat, either – but it did. We were then taken to stay the night at our best friend's house, away from the turmoil at home.

When we went back home the following day, it seemed calmer than the day before. There were lots of people around; some were in the kitchen, some were eating. Just the murmur of low, hushed voices could be heard now. In the main living room, cleared of all furniture, a Granthi (Sikh priest) chanted prayers.

Early that evening, I realized no one was with Dad. He was lying on a bed in the study. In that quiet moment, I crept into the room. I wanted to see him, to touch him to see if he was any warmer.

Then I remembered what the missionaries had said at school, when they'd talked about Lazarus being brought back to life. Four days after Lazarus' death, Jesus called him from his tomb and he walked again. As a child, you believed what anyone in authority told you. I really believed in the miracle of Lazarus and the missionaries had such conviction that it was possible to bring the dead back to life, so surely it must be true – right? The missionaries said that if we prayed hard enough and truly believed, God would answer our prayers. Well, I believed! I believed that if I prayed hard enough to Jesus, He'd bring my dad back to life. I resolved to do it there and then.

The air turned ice-cold. I tried to pray but couldn't make a sound. There was a presence in that room and it spoke menacingly.

'If he wakes up, he'll choke the life out of you.' The male voice was deep, guttural. 'Remember the beating you had? That's nothing compared to what he'll do to you now. You'll die this time.'

I could feel the hairs on the back of my neck stand up. I was rigid. All I could sense was a swirling around me – a darkness, a malevolence, and a feeling of foreboding I'll never forget to this day. I gave my beloved father one last stricken look and fled.

I later wondered if I should have said that prayer to defeat what was surely an evil presence. The missionaries at school had said that if we called upon Jesus or said 'Get thee behind me, Satan, in the name of Jesus,' when we had a bad thought or were afraid, then we'd be freed of the thought or the fear. I felt ashamed that I'd allowed fear to overpower me to such a degree that I wouldn't risk death to save my father. I felt he'd done everything he could to save me, not just by adopting me, but also in his quest to seek a cure for me, and yet I couldn't even utter a prayer to bring him back to life. At least, that's the way I understood it as a ten-year-old. I berated myself for being so weak. I don't know if it was just part of the grieving process, but that guilt lay heavily upon me and I never spoke of it to anyone – not until now, in this book.

I'll never fully be able to understand why I had that experience. I've considered that the voice may have been a projection of the shock and grief at losing Dad, warning me not to interfere with matters of life and death. Perhaps the voice, that guttural menace, was trying to protect me from the inevitable disappointment at not being able to bring him back to life. Or maybe the devil was in that room at that time, instilling fear. I will never be sure. What I do know, with total clarity, is that I was rescued. My legs were paralysed in shock, but I felt arms around my waist, pulling me away.

I now know this was my guardian angel. I have never felt such fear, yet I found the strength in my legs to run. That wasn't my strength – I know that I had a Divine helper with me. As with the guilt of not praying for Dad, I told no one about my encounter with my angel. I was too frightened that people would laugh at me, because at the time I, too, found that episode confusing.

I didn't cry when they took Dad away for cremation, but those tears came a week later when a boy came up to me at school and said simply, 'Your dad was a really good man. I'm sorry. Everyone respected him.'

I hid behind a tree in the school garden and cried. Those words finally brought home to me the fact that he'd really gone and that he'd been so well regarded. In their eyes, he had value.

I still mourn the loss of my fearless father, the hunter whose trained eye detected the first flicker of danger from wild animals on those safari days he took me on. The dad who taught me to shoot 'in case I needed to protect myself', ignoring my mother's scolding that he mustn't teach girls those things. I sense him now in the jungle or in the safari park with his gun, ready to defend us, primed to teach us the ways of each and every animal. He may have hunted, but he also respected the animals. As I mentioned earlier, he'd never have *chosen* to deliberately kill animals such as the eland or blackbuck antelopes, as he believed them to be directly related to cows, which are deemed sacred in Hinduism. And he couldn't bear killing for the sake of it, just to take the lives of animals as trophies – it was important to Dad that the animals he hunted were for food purposes only, the meat from which he often shared throughout our village.

I cried under the tree that day, thinking of how Dad always defended those in need of help. How one time he'd waded into a baying crowd of angry people with clubs and raised fists. A thief had stolen a loaf of bread – that's all it took for a throng to gather in front of Dad's garage, yelling for justice. Dad was shouting at them to stop, but he knew they wouldn't until the man had been stoned, kicked and beaten to death. Dad offered to pay the baker for the bread, but they were acting like enraged buffaloes, their eyes screaming death – in their eyes, only death would do.

Dad waded in and grabbed the man from the furious crowd. Then he dragged him through the garage doors, ordering the workers to bar the doors behind them. The workers did as they were told, but I could see in their eyes a sullen resentment. They, too, believed the thief should be killed. Still, the mob of men, women and children bellowed and shouted, baying for the thief's blood.

My father asked for a bowl of water to tend the man's wounds, but all the servants and workers melted away, not wanting any part in saving a thief's life. My mum provided the bowl of water and made a turmeric paste for my dad to apply to the man's wounds. '*Santa sana, santa sana,*' the man repeated. 'Thank you, thank you.' He knew my dad had saved his life.

When the police came to arrest the man, Dad slipped a piece of paper into his hand.

'This is my telephone number. When you come out of jail, call me and I'll get you a job. Don't come here – it's too dangerous. If they recognize you out there, they'll kill you.'

The man nodded his gratitude. Dad meant it. The same way as he had when he'd taken in other young men and given them work, paid for their training and supported their families, hoping they'd be able to make something of their lives someday.

Under the tree that day, I wept for the father who'd celebrated the birth of his daughters and my adoption, ignoring the taunts of society. 'No one celebrates the birth of daughters and offers *laddoos*.' Those sweets were only brought out to celebrate the birth of sons. (Some of the Indian community even went so far as to say that people only celebrated the births of females because they'd grow up to be prostitutes and bring in money.) My father didn't care. As far as he was concerned, we were just as precious as the boys.

I mourned the dad who spent hours reading stories to us when we were younger, desperate for us to learn English like the Queen of England. He was a patient dad who tried so hard to teach me to say the letter 'w', when all I could say was 'bubloo'. I looked at the sign above our school – 'Kabale Preparatory' – and remembered the fees my dad had paid to get us, his three daughters, educated. His words reverberated in my head: 'I want you to be educated. To become something. Become a lawyer, become a doctor, whatever. I believe you can all do it.' Typical Indian careers, I know, but in those days, my dad was unique in wanting not only his sons, but also his daughters, to have a profession.

Some years later, I was to take his advice. While my path wasn't to be one of law or medicine, I did train in social work, as did my sister, of which I know he'd be proud. And it was because of him and the sacrifices he made against society that I was able to do so.

I lamented the dad who spent hours tending to my sores, the dad who spent hours driving hundreds of miles, travelling the length and breadth of Uganda to explore even a slim possibility of a cure for my epidermolysis bullosa. He spent thousands and never accepted the dire prediction that I wouldn't live to be a teenager. Sadly, many people do die of this rare disease, but Dad believed I'd survive.

I grieved for the dad who took us with him when he went to meet his friends at the weekends in the White Horse Inn in Kabale. They'd gather in front of a roaring log fire, and now and again Dad would call us over to introduce us to passing visitors, naming each of us with a fierce pride. When he introduced me and was met with questioning eyes, he'd gaze back and just repeat, 'My daughter, my Bharti.' There was something in his look that quelled any further questions from strangers.

This was the dad who wasn't ashamed to show the world how much he held all of us in his worth. Precious moments and equally precious memories held forever in our hearts and minds.

In my younger days, I lived in the shadow of the beating from Dad and the uncertainty of him sending me away. It was this that stopped me from fully expressing my love for my dad and from telling him how much he meant to me, marring our relationship. I guess I was afraid of doing or saying something that might lead to my removal from the family home, my position tenuous. Then with my illness came the rebuilding of our relationship, so out of something bad came something good. But the reality is that those two incidents constituted such a small percentage of our lives together as father and daughter. The rest of the time, he was a fantastic dad.

It took my dad's death for me to see his true worth and I only wish I could have expressed how I felt to him before he died. If my dad had still been alive, I'd have said to him, 'This is how I felt when you beat me.' Then I'd have asked him to tell me about it. 'Tell me what drove you to it.' I then wish I could have said to him, 'Dad, I forgive you for that.'

But as life went on and my epidermolysis bullosa took over, I never got that chance. I guess he showed his guilt and remorse in the way he took care of me. In our own way, we made peace with one another, but I wish we'd been able to express it, to voice it aloud. I once overheard Dad saying to Mum, 'Her blisters are God's way of punishing me because of what I did. I should never have hit her.' In his own way he was trying to say, 'I'm sorry.' But he needn't have been – for he wasn't the cause.

The dad I knew had been defeated by death and that forlorn day, hidden in the trees, I wept unrelentingly for both my loss and that of my family. He was just 52 years old and Mum had become a widow at 40. I desperately wanted him back and knew nothing would ever be the same.

Mum had to make the decision, alone, to leave Uganda. Given the growing danger, she decided we had no choice but to go. There were many stories of girls of very young ages being forced to marry soldiers or being raped by them. Much pressure was put on Mum to change our destination from England to India, as we had more family there to support us. Mum was told that in England she'd be isolated and that she'd have no one to turn to. She was also advised that it wasn't a good country in which to bring up girls, as we'd be morally corrupted by English ways. But Mum knew she needed to get treatment for my epidermolysis bullosa from Dr Emerson and stood firm in her resolve that we were going to England come what may. That had been Dad's dream – and she had to make it come true.

~

CHAPTER 7

Mothers' Courage

'If I find one more cent in these belongings, I promise I'll shoot you dead here and now.'

The soldier is staring at my brother, Shankerdas. Our suitcases are open on the roadside and soldiers are rifling through my brother's things – two cents had fallen out of his clothes and we were praying the soldiers wouldn't find more.

One of the conditions that Idi Amin had imposed when asking Asians to leave the country was that no one could have money in their possession, regardless of the amount, the President believing Asians had exploited Ugandan people enough. They didn't need any excuse when it came to shooting people for stealing, even just cents (equivalent to pennies), so we'd been under strict instructions not to travel with any money at all. It was such a tiny amount, just forgotten about and left in a trouser pocket. Surely my brother wouldn't die for that?

Asian families heading for Kampala from towns outside were forced out of their cars and onto the roadside while their vehicle and luggage were systematically searched. The soldiers took anything they found for themselves. Some families never even made it to Kampala and rumours of girls being taken by soldiers, never to be seen again, were rife. Because it was a distinct possibility, in some cases girls were dressed as boys. Some had their hair cut and others had their hair tied in buns with turbans placed on their heads. Either that or they had buns knotted in a handkerchief, so they looked like Sikh boys – all so they wouldn't be abducted, raped and killed. My mother contemplated doing the same to my sisters and me but changed her mind, believing that if other families ahead of us had already done it and were found out, it might actually be worse for us should we be stopped.

We waited in the blistering sun as the search continued. No more coins rolled out and I was reaching the conclusion that surely they'd let us drive on now. Instead, I realized the soldier's gun was now pointing at my mother and we were mute with fear, the deafening sound I could hear merely my heart pulsating in terror.

'Leave her here,' he ordered, glancing at me briefly. 'She's one of us.'

Time stopped. On the roadside, the heat shimmied and danced in front of us, defying the gravity of our situation, a feeling of dread setting in.

'Leave her here.' The soldier's eyes were bloodshot and full of hate.

My mother kept her gaze lowered, demonstrating her deference. Looking at him directly would have antagonized him further.

'But I can't leave her here. She's mine.'

I stared ahead. From the corner of my eye, I could see his gun still pointing at her chest.

'I said, she's one of us. What use could you possibly have for her where you're going?' The soldier's voice was now raised and he looked as if he was about to step forwards menacingly.

Still gazing down, Mum was adamant when she replied. 'If we leave, we leave with her. I'm *not* leaving her behind.'

Mr M, the taxi driver who was waiting for us to get back in the car so we could continue to Kampala, shot a glance at her. I could see he was alarmed, no doubt wondering if she was mad, arguing with a man who was holding a loaded gun in his hand. He moved quickly to one side to distance himself from us, to make it clear he wasn't one of us. He evidently didn't want to be shot – and certainly not for one little girl.

'I said, leave her behind!' the soldier repeated.

Mum gave him the briefest of looks and lowered her head once more. 'Sorry, sir, but I can't do that. She's my child, just like all the others. She's as precious to me as all of my children.'

He cocked the trigger.

No one moved. It was hard to breathe. From the corner of my eye, I saw that Mr M was wiping his forehead, sweat streaming down his face. All six of us were standing on the road in a perfect firing line. My mother, Shankerdas, my two sisters, me. My baby brother was in my mother's arms. The last thing we needed was for him to start crying now.

As we waited for the soldier's decision, I recited the Lord's Prayer the missionaries had taught us: 'Our Father, who art in heaven....' I couldn't remember the rest, despite reciting it every day at school, so I kept repeating the little I could recall over and over. 'Our Father, who art in heaven...'.

Suddenly, the solider laughed. He threw back his head and actually laughed! He lowered his gun, pointing the muzzle at the ground. Then came what I took to be a grudging look of respect – or was it admiration?

'Okay, you can go. I salute your courage.' He nodded to my mother. 'Take her and go,' he said with a dismissive wave of his hand towards me. 'I'll radio ahead to tell my comrades to leave you alone.'

'Thank you, thank you,' breathed my mother gratefully as she herded us back into the waiting taxi.

Mr M jumped into the driver's seat, still sweating profusely. Yet, there was no sense of relief – for all we knew this soldier could still change his mind. As might the next soldier down the road.

Mr M gave the soldier a nervous smile and edged the car forwards. We all stared ahead resolutely, not daring to make eye contact. Eye contact was dangerous. It showed disrespect, and could make any soldier mad and start shooting.

As the car picked up speed, still we didn't feel safe. We were waiting for the first bullets to rip into the taxi directed from the soldiers manning the roadblock we'd just left behind. Sitting behind Mum, I fixed my gaze on the back of her head. I could have asked her, 'Why did that soldier say I wasn't yours?' I knew the answer, of course, but she still had no idea that I'd found out about my adoption. The soldier was referring to my dual heritage, being of Asian-African descent. That's why he'd said I was one of them – referring to my African roots. But maybe now wasn't the time to ask about it. An inner voice said she'd been through enough, and also I didn't want Mr M to hear me asking such questions.

Mr M glanced over at my mother. 'My God, Mama,' he said. 'I thought the end had come for all of you – us, even, with me included.'

She kept looking straight ahead and smiled. 'I knew nothing was going to happen. Goddess Lakshmi was with me and told me we'd be leaving Uganda. Their father also came in a dream and confirmed that we were going to be safe.'

Mum's refusal to leave me behind made me feel so precious. She was prepared to sacrifice not just her life, but that of the whole family, too, for the sake of one. I was overwhelmed at the feeling of being truly valued, truly loved, and that I was worth dying for.

That wasn't the only risk Mum had taken for me that proved her extraordinary courage, either. For when we were stationary at the roadblock, waiting in turn to be searched, a soldier had taken a wheelchair from the car in front of us and hurled it down the hill – a child's wheelchair belonging to a young boy with a disability. A family with three or four children had stood helplessly by their car. Shankerdas, who was 14 at the time – I was 12 years old – later told me that a soldier had shot the disabled child. It's strange how the mind works. We'd all witnessed this scene and yet I'd refused to believe it. I think my mind blocked it out as it was too horrific. I preferred to think that I'd seen just the wheelchair being thrown down the hill – it was the only way to protect my mind from the sheer horror of the alternative.

This same soldier had inevitably asked the same questions of the child's parents as he had of my mother. Why are you taking him? What use is he where you're going?

After the soldier had killed the boy, we overheard the soldier saying to the mother, 'I've done good, haven't I, Mama?'

Her husband said to her in the language of Gujarati, 'Just nod and say yes.'

She had to do it, for there was little choice. I imagine it must have been difficult for those parents to have kept all of their grief and shock inside.

It was common for parents to recount experiences they'd faced with the soldiers once safe in the refugee camps, and we later heard that the father of the disabled child had had a complete breakdown when they'd arrived at the airport in the UK and that he'd had to be hospitalized. It seemed to us children listening in on these conversations that there had been many other families where various family members had 'gone mad' on reaching the UK and been taken away for treatment.

Mum had witnessed that terrible scene just moments before it was our turn – I can only imagine what she must have been thinking. How she managed to defy him is beyond me to this day, knowing what he was capable of. Because we were directly behind them in the queue, there was nowhere else to look. And worse still, the same lead soldier with the bloodshot eyes who'd intimidated Mum was the one who'd shot that defenceless child. My mother had seen him murder that boy with her own eyes, then approach our car, after which he'd asked her to leave me behind, no doubt like he'd asked the family before to leave the disabled child. The threat to my life and to all of us would have been very real.

When I look back at that time, I know how much my mother surrendered to her faith in the Divine. She'd capitulated, knowing there could only be four outcomes: the soldier would either let us go, or he'd kill her, me or potentially all of us. I also sense that our guardian angels must have worked hard to ensure our whole family's protection when our lives hung by a thread. I know angels protected me that day, just like when I was found as an abandoned baby. Those two miracles both occurred by a roadside – one on the outskirts of Kabale and the other 100 km (60-odd miles) from Kabale on the road to Kampala. For me, roadsides came to symbolize decisions that meant life or death, and one where angels came to the rescue.

We travelled the 480 km (300 miles) to Kampala, the Ugandan capital, facing roadblocks every 80 km (50 miles), soldiers searching both cars and occupants on each occasion. Mr M was the only man in Kabale who still had a car, probably because he'd married a Ugandan woman, as instructed by Idi Amin, and the soldiers respected him for his inter-racial relationship, thereby proving he truly was an integrated Ugandan citizen in their eyes. All other vehicles had been confiscated by the soldiers.

We weren't the first family to escape from the town thanks to Mr M's taxi. He made a vow to drive day and night with just a few hours' rest so all of the Asian families stranded in Kabale would be able to leave within the 45-day deadline. All he asked was that each family be ready to leave at a moment's notice if he knocked on their door.

We became part of a convoy as cars from other towns headed along the same route. Asians from other towns hadn't had their cars confiscated like us, so many more cars joined us on that deadly exodus. Kabale had been targeted merely because of its location on the Congo–Rwandan border to prevent people from fleeing into Rwanda and Congo, or 'spies' from those regions using vehicles against Idi Amin and his notorious regime.

As children, we might not have understood the full extent of the danger we were in, but we were in no doubt that it was Mum's prayers offered to Mataji (Mother Goddess) that assured the goddess' Divine protection on our journey to Kampala. Her palpable relief said it all.

Our place of refuge in Kampala had an air of hasty abandonment about it. It was my aunt and uncle's house and it had negative associations for me. The last time we'd needed putting up there, before I was admitted to Mulago Hospital for tests, my aunt had apologetically but firmly told Dad that she didn't want her children – my cousins – catching my skin disease. For that reason, she'd misguidedly banned us from staying there overnight. We'd automatically assumed they'd take us in, but when she said we couldn't stay, Dad refused to share even so much as a drink or a snack with them. He'd given them shelter when they'd first arrived from India, only for us to be rejected because of their misplaced fear of contagion.

Instead, Dad and I were forced to stay with another family. They weren't relatives, but the welcome we received was so loving and their acceptance of me so unconditional that tears welled within me. I'd been so worried that Dad would have nowhere to stay because of me. I'd got used to rejection rather than acceptance from strangers, so it was a sweet shock when I met people who didn't shy away. But for him to have to face rejection because of me was too much to bear and I felt an overwhelming sense of guilt. To me, this other family were all angels in human form. It just showed that there are times when friends we choose are worth more than the relatives we don't choose. They say you can choose your friends but not your relatives, but I know this isn't the case and that you can choose your relatives, too.

Stepping into my aunt and uncle's empty house that terrifying day brought back sad memories of rejection – but then I remembered the other family who had been so loving. Another angel in disguise was the courageous Mr M. I don't know if he escaped Uganda with his life or not, but I sincerely hope he and his family are safe now.

We were joined at the house a day or so later by Pritam Paaji (Dad's nephew, who lived in Kabale) and Bhabiji, his wife. They'd originally planned to leave for the airport the day before us, but he'd changed his departure date to leave after us so he could be sure we'd left safely. He said he owed it to his uncle, my dad, to ensure we were safe. I recall Bhabiji being a very strict but loving second mum to us all. She had four children who came to call me aunty. At that time, though, we simply wondered if we'd survive long enough even to reach the airport.

Mum and Pritam Paaji went into Kampala to fetch the papers we'd need for our departure, leaving us with Bhabiji for a couple of days. During the day we could play freely but with firm orders to stay in front of the house and not wander off. But just before sunset, we'd scuttle back inside. It was important to show that the house was unoccupied, so every evening one of my cousin's children or my brother would climb out of a window, lock the door from the outside and then climb back in through the window. A chain and heavy padlock on the front door gave a sure outward sign that the house was empty, hopefully keeping the soldiers away.

During our evening meal, we were given instructions to remain completely silent if there was a knock on the door. We weren't to make a sound, not even a cough. All lights needed to be off and we were to lie on top of our beds in complete darkness. If soldiers started breaking down the door, we were all to climb into the water tank in the bathroom. Again – we weren't to make a sound, no matter how cold the water. We were worried that we'd drown, but Bhabiji reassured us the water wasn't that deep. She said she'd knock three times on the tank when it was safe to come out. We had no idea how long it would be before we could venture out, or what would happen if her knocks didn't come. As children, we just accepted it.

Once darkness fell, we all slept in one room, but we were told not to climb into bed. If we had to bolt, Bhabiji didn't want the beds to look slept in, so we lay on top of the quilts, with instructions to smooth them swiftly if the need arose. Not a whisper was to be heard.

Then came the awful trundling sound of a truck coming up the road that we'd so dreaded. It stopped outside our house and we tensed, ready to flee into the water tank.

Soldiers began pounding on the neighbour's door, where we knew a young couple with twins was living. Through the wall, we could hear the soldiers entering their home and shouting abuse at the family. The babies woke up with the commotion and one of them began to cry.

'Shut it up!' a soldier commanded.

The mother attempted to quieten a child who wouldn't hush. Then the other twin started blubbing.

'Shut them up now, or I'll do it for you,' the soldier shouted.

'But they're babies. Babies cry. Don't you have children?' the mother retorted.

Two shots rang out. The babies' cries were silenced immediately. The parents started screaming and wailing. Two more shots. Silence.

We heard the bodies being dragged out of the house, followed by a cry of, 'Throw them into the lorry. The crocodiles will be happy today.' There was raucous laughter at that.

Bhabiji put her finger to her lips and her eyes conveyed a stern warning: don't so much as make a move – there was to be complete silence as they still hadn't left. The chain on the front door rattled moments later and the soldiers knocked repeatedly on our door.

'Looks like this lot have gone,' one said.

Footsteps faded. Then we heard the truck start up and move away, struggling with its heavy load of death.

Sleep came uneasily that night and we slept fitfully, waking at the slightest noise in case the soldiers came back to check that our house really was empty.

The next day, we woke late. Bhabiji refused to let us out in case someone was watching the house. We heard the tinkling bell of the man with the ice-cream trolley coming up the road – how we longed for an ice cream.... But Bhabiji said it might be a trap – it could be a soldier trying to see who was left in the street. There was to be no ice cream or fun that day. She only had to remind us sharply about the deaths of the people next door when we complained about not being allowed out to play.

I only realized when I was older how big a sacrifice Bhabiji had been prepared to make both for her children and for us. If the soldiers had entered the house, we might have been safely ensconced in the tank, but anything could have happened to her. She could have been raped then shot and her body taken to the river – anything. The older children might have realized the sacrifices she made, but the younger ones certainly wouldn't have appreciated her courage. I remember hearing her call upon her faith to get us through that night when the soldiers came and took the lives of the family next door. And I remember her prayer-bead necklace, which she used to hold when praying in meditation each morning and evening.

Mum arrived back at the house the following day, exhausted. The queues at the visa office had been long and it had taken nearly two days of waiting in the searing heat to secure the papers that would permit us to leave. They'd slept fitfully on a bench the first night while awaiting their turn until my mum had fainted the following day just before the office was due to be closed. When Paaji explained she was diabetic, they were instructed to come to the front of the queue. Paaji explained that they'd still have been waiting in the queue for a third day had it not been for Mum fainting.

A day later, Pritam Paaji had arranged for a taxi to take us to Entebbe International Airport, some 80 km (50 miles) away. Not even the fear of what the next night would bring quelled my mounting excitement about the journey to come. I was going to board a plane for the first time and land in a strange country, where we'd be starting our new life – one of freedom!

It is now that I sense the tremendous courage of mothers at times of adversity. Bhabiji had been prepared to die to save her children, nephews and nieces, while my mother was equally prepared to make the ultimate sacrifice: to save me or die trying alongside the rest of her family. Faith is a powerful force. Mum's faith told her we weren't destined to die that day, but it still takes courage to accept the message and to trust in it fully. I was terrified at the ways in which people died and it was that fear of suffering that was much greater than any horror of death itself. We'd been brought up to believe in reincarnation so, to us, death wasn't the final chapter, just the start of a new life. But this wasn't our time to die. We had to trust in Mum's belief that we'd make it to the airport and that our lives would continue.

Faith empowers us to know that we're not alone in a battle for survival. It helps us to get through moments of darkness, anger or despair. Mum's faith guided both her and us throughout.

~

CHAPTER 8

Escape

We were ordered to disembark, to stand in line on the hot tarmac and wait. Having never been on a plane before, I believed this must be part of the normal routine when it came to flying – just like it had been each time we took off, flew for a few minutes, then turned around and made the descent back into Entebbe. You think you're free and safe, and then the procedure starts all over again as you're forced to return, only to undergo yet more checks, more soldiers.

Eventually, we were ordered back onto the plane and, once again, the neat queue on the tarmac became a disorderly rush for seats in the aircraft cabin. With no seat allocation, it was mayhem – parents frantically calling and searching for their children and partners so they could sit together for the long flight. My Mum, panic-stricken, ended up losing my youngest sister, Mina. Mum had given Mina to Shankerdas to look after when we were waiting to get back on board with instructions to hold her hand and not let go. I was carrying Shiv and Anju was holding Mum's hand.

In the desperate rush for seats, Shankerdas had had let go of Mina's hand and we realized Mina was missing when Mum came to check on us once the melee had settled, just when the plane was about to take off again. Mum was beside herself – hysterical, even. The stewardess was shouting at her to take her seat, but my mum wouldn't listen, frantically calling for Mina and asking Shankerdas where he'd left her and when he last saw her. Mum yelled at the crew that they couldn't possibly set off as her daughter had been left behind.

But the airline staff were firm: 'We're leaving and we're leaving now, with or without her.'

Mum eventually located Mina, who was sitting with strangers right at the back of the plane, completely oblivious to our fear that she'd been left behind. Mum marched her to her seat next to us, grasping her hand tightly. There would be no more disappearances – or so we thought.

We took off twice more, only to land once again. The second and third time, soldiers came aboard searching for a particular passenger, whom they arrested and marched off the plane. No one knew whether those passengers were to be imprisoned, tortured or shot. But whatever was destined to happen to them after being dragged off, it was too hard to contemplate right then, especially after what we'd been through when we'd first arrived at the airport when going through security. We'd been stopped and Mum was wearing her gold jewellery, having been told by the taxi driver on the way to Kampala not to stow it in the suitcases. Apparently, the soldiers would have killed us if they'd found it, believing we were trying to smuggle things out of the country, so Mum had been left with no option but to wear it.

One of the soldiers, a female officer, had ordered Mum take it all off and hand it over, leaving her no choice but to remove her necklaces, rings and bangles and place them on the counter. When Mum started crying, something miraculous happened: the soldier wrapped all the jewellery in a handkerchief and pushed the little bundle back towards my mother.

'Don't you dare tell anybody about this. Put it away now,' she whispered, standing to one side so that her colleagues wouldn't see Mum slip it into her handbag. 'If you're caught with this again, you're not to tell them I gave it back to you.'

When nobody else checked our bags after that, it became apparent that my mother's prayers had been answered. She'd dreamed that we'd leave Uganda safely and she'd maintained absolute faith that we'd all be protected throughout.

If it hadn't been for the decision of that soldier, we'd have arrived in the UK with nothing but the clothes in which we stood up. It hadn't been possible to sell my father's garage before we left because the government had put restrictions on the sale of Asian businesses, such was Idi Amin's determination that no money should leave the country and that everything belonged to Uganda. The short space of time in which he gave Asians to leave the country would have made any sale impossible in any case. The gold was all we had and there were five mouths to feed. (At that time, we weren't aware that the UK had a benefit system, and in Indian culture gold gave security so that if you were ever in need, you'd have something to sell or trade.)

Looking back, that female official's leniency was extraordinary, especially when the belief was that Asians had exploited native African Ugandans. The majority of Africans worked in low-level positions in Ugandan society with little economic power, while Asian businesses thrived. But my father never abused his position as a business owner and gave generously to those who needed help in terms of money, education or employment. However, he couldn't change the racial hierarchy alone. And he wasn't with us then, there at the airport, praying with his family that we'd reach England – or at least not in person, though perhaps in spirit.

At last, the plane announcement came granting permission to leave the country once again. Hope filled our hearts as we buckled our seat belts and prepared for take-off. From the cabin windows we could see military personnel on the ground, guns at the ready. As the engines powered up and we taxied along the runway, they shrank to the size of toy soldiers. My fear ebbed and my excitement revved up with the roar of the plane's engines as we headed into our unknown future once again.

When the plane began to descend, I automatically assumed we were back in Uganda once more and that the soldiers were going to come back onboard to forcibly evict another poor soul. So it was with relief that I realized we'd landed in England. We'd flown for nine hours, during which time I must have slept throughout, as it had felt like no time at all. We weren't back where we'd started. We'd arrived in the UK!

Tears of relief and prayers of thanks could be heard by all, and all the adults were cheering. We were safe, in England at last. Mum, however, didn't feel the same way, relief far from her mind. I often wonder at her strength during those critical hours. She'd managed that terrifying exodus as the sole responsible adult without my father alongside her – and we'd all lived to tell the tale. I just wish my father had been with us and that we'd left much sooner. Would he still have been alive? I'll never know....

Stepping out of the plane in light summer clothes in the cold London air brought with it a sensation of being bitten all over my body. *Had another skin ailment flared up?* Anxiously, I checked my bare arms.

'Can you feel it?' I whispered to Anju.

But she could feel it, too, and that was when I came to understand what the term 'biting cold' meant, for that was the sensation we felt right then.

Some helpers offered us blankets and we wrapped them around us like shawls, grateful for protection not just from the cold, but also from the fear we'd felt during our ordeal to flee Uganda.

Then came the blur of questions as we filled out copious forms, then coaches lined up to take us away to goodness knows where. In the distance, I glimpsed crowds of people waving placards and shouting. At the time, I didn't understand why they were there – and I'm so glad of that now. It's as if that cloak of protection in the form of a blanket had distracted us from the protestors and all we could hear was the din of our own excited chatter. We were safe – and we had a chance to make a new start, each and every one of us. We resolved to learn everything we needed to in order to fit in quickly.

The coach driver was a very kind man who took us on a little tour around London first before taking us to the camp (*the land of Dick*

Whittington – oh joy!). As soon as we took our seats, he went round closing all the curtains, instructing us to keep them shut until we were out of Heathrow. It was only later that we realized the crowd were National Front supporters, angry at our arrival. The coach driver didn't want us to witness that hatred, not when we were so buoyant, no doubt having left all sorts of horrors behind us.

We sped away from the airport, and when the driver gave us his cue we drew back the curtains and gazed into an inky, murky London sky. The dazzling lights of the capital made us feel excited about a city we might get to know one day. But I was disappointed that the roads looked so dirty, having imagined them to be clean and pristine. We'd been led to believe from the children of the missionaries that England was white and clean, with not one bit of rubbish or speck of dirt to be seen anywhere, so it came as a surprise to see otherwise. But we still believed in the story of Dick Whittington, and despite the fact the streets weren't paved with gold, somehow we were convinced that they actually were. 'They have to be dirty,' one learned young man said importantly. 'Underneath those stones, there's real gold. It's dirty on top to stop the thieves from stealing it.'

I wondered if those dashing through those streets were aware of our presence on the coach – a group of refugees from a faraway land. I saw a couple laughing as they ran across the road and their happy, smiling faces lifted my heart. Their smiles were infectious and I realized how much I had to smile about now, for there were no soldiers here, no guns to worry about – just the cold that bit into our skin. But that was a tiny price to pay for freedom. I thanked God, grateful for the coach driver who, to me, was giving us a mystery tour of London, giving us a taste of what freedom looked like.

It was dark when we arrived at the camp on Greenham Common in Berkshire. Row upon row of grey beds had been lined up on the airbase still manned by American soldiers, though the only time we saw a soldier or two was when we left or entered the base. These soldiers had guns, too, reminding us of harder times. Some of the children and adults were terrified of them and we all kept clear. It was hard to trust, given what we'd witnessed and experienced first-hand. For me, believing them all to be potential killers, soldiers came to represent people who didn't value the lives of other human beings.

We'd assumed one side of the dormitory, with its dozen beds, was ours but soon realized our mistake when more families arrived in the following days. When another family arrived a few days later, one of the camp officials told us we had six beds allocated to us, but we'd spread our belongings across 12 beds! We'd have to get used to sharing.

There was a large boundary fence around the airbase, but we were suddenly free to explore wherever we liked – from wandering into the woods (during daylight hours) to visiting the gigantic canteen where all of our meals were served. Then there was the laundry room, too, where Mum could wash and dry our clothes. We were agog at the huge machines and offered to help her. Mum and the other parents looked on with amusement that we were so eager. We were even given coats, unfamiliar garments with a wonderful ability to keep out the biting cold and wind.

On Thursday evenings, a large crowd of youths would gather in one room. This was where the television was, the hub of excitement, the allure of learning about the world beyond the camp prevalent.

On *Top of the Pops*, a boy was singing that he was a long-haired lover from Liverpool and that he'd be someone's long-haired lover. Mum didn't understand, but one word stood out for her: lover. Horrified, she'd urged us out of the room and told us, in no uncertain terms, that the TV room was now out of bounds. The only one allowed to stay was Shankerdas – and boy did he gloat about it! Mum made sure the rest of us stayed in on Thursday evenings from that day forwards, but to us it was still freedom. For we stayed in knowing we were safe. No soldiers patrolling outside our dormitories, waiting to kill. There was freedom to talk, to play and to laugh without fear or tension.

I loved the refugee camp and particularly Urvashi, who became my best friend. She and I became friendly with the camp policeman, who became known as Uncle Tom. We'd shriek his name whenever we passed his little station and he'd wave back at us. It was very strange to us that he didn't carry a gun, as it was normal for the police in Uganda to carry weapons. The police in Kabale always looked like they were on official business and would never have smiled and waved at us, so we were somewhat intrigued by Uncle Tom, who was unlike any policeman we'd ever seen in Uganda. We quickly decided he was safe to be around and he always seemed to be on duty. Sometimes he'd be occupied with paperwork and wouldn't look up, or we'd see him talking severely to some sullen young man or other, but mostly he waved and smiled. Such a welcome contrast to what we were used to!

A school opened at the camp and our carefree days of running about, exploring, annoying canteen staff and fetching delicious milk from the machine were suddenly over as studying became our new focus. We loved playing with the other children, but when we returned to our dormitories it was as if we barely knew each other.

When we'd first arrived, the few families already there had marked their territory by placing a small barrier of suitcases around their sleeping areas. Their little space, their little home, no doubt. It seemed the families wanted a clear demarcation that whatever space they had was their home – as if there were some invisible door or wall between our spaces. It was almost as if we were forbidden from trespassing, if you like, from going over to play and chat. It was a very strange situation, but all the adults in our block adopted this stance. I guess it was the only control they had over a situation in which they had no real say about anything – although to us it was still freedom.

As children, we didn't understand this and excitedly went up to one family, introducing ourselves. But their mother turned to her children and said sharply that they weren't to speak to us, before turning away from us, clearly signalling that we shouldn't just turn up uninvited. Yet, we could see them from our beds.

Back in Uganda, people were generally very friendly with each other. No one had sought permission to play with someone, visit someone or speak to them, but this family clearly didn't want to be associated with us. Mum explained that they were in their place and we were in ours, and that we needed to respect their wishes and wait to be invited into their area. It was clear we had a lot of learning to do now we were in England.

In Indian culture, when you wanted to visit someone, you simply knocked on their door. But in England, it seemed, we'd have to learn we needed to make an appointment first. Our models for this behaviour were the English missionaries we'd grown up with in Uganda, who were sticklers for formality, and if we wanted to see them, we'd have to make an appointment. I recall my mother saying we had to behave properly and to be like them.

English ideas and etiquette were quickly adopted in other areas in the camp as well, and it became clear people didn't want to connect with each other. Knowing we'd be separated when the housing allocation began, the adults believed there was no point getting attached. While we children played together at school, at home in the dormitories we had to pretend we were invisible to each other.

The adults were to be proved right. While Urvashi and I were firm friends in the camp, we never saw each other again – nor any of the other families we'd met there. Looking back, we'd risked our lives to get to the UK and no one had anything left to give of themselves. Rather than bond together, people took refuge in separation.

My sister Mina made a friend in camp, too. One evening, she asked if she could go to her friend's house (by 'house', she meant dormitory). Unlike some of the families housed with us, her parents were fine with Mina playing with their daughter, so Mum agreed that she could go.

When Mina didn't return that night, Shankerdas and Mum went to the friend's dormitory only to find Mina had disappeared. The family said she'd left their dormitory earlier and as far as they were concerned, she'd gone straight home to us. An hour had passed since she'd left, so it was now dark, given it was November.

Mum went straight to Uncle Tom, who put a search party together. The next minute, helicopters were hovering above us and police dogs were barking on leads as what felt like an army of police searched the camp and the woods nearby. It was winter, so it was cold and dark, and we could see the glint of their flashlights as they combed every inch of the area looking for our lost sister.

Mum was beside herself until the early hours of the morning, when the police eventually found Mina hiding under her friend's bed. The girls had devised a plan whereby Mina would stay the night and then, the next day, the two of them would fly back to Uganda. They'd decided that they'd sneak out of the camp in the early hours of the morning when everyone was asleep and try to find a plane to take them back. At the time, this made complete sense to six-year-old Mina, who was still grieving for Dad and believed she'd find him back in Kabale, where he'd look after her.

She was slapped soundly by Mum and told in no uncertain terms that she was never going to be allowed to visit friends again. It was then Mina broke down and told us she missed Uganda and Dad and that she wanted to go home. Mum wrapped her in her arms and comforted her. We all had to accept the change in our lives, but she was too young to understand the idea of separation and the permanence of death. Soon, though, the lesson of how we needed to accept change was to come to us all.

We'd got back home from school one day to find a woman named Aunty Margaret sitting on the bed with Mum. Aunty Margaret had visited several times to help Mum with my youngest brother, Shiv, who was two years old. He was to be assigned a health visitor, Aunty Margaret, until he was five. We'd never heard of health visitors before and came to learn how brilliant this country was to have such systems in place designed to help families. She was the kindest woman we knew. Whenever she visited, she brought sweets or chocolates for us. Sometimes she'd bring clothes, too.

Mum told us that she wasn't well and that she had to go to hospital. She gave us a weak smile and said that she'd be okay, but something didn't feel right. The last time someone in our family had been to hospital, they hadn't returned, and this was at the forefront of my mind. We were to be placed with a family who were to look after us until she was well enough to return.

There was another woman there as well, who introduced herself as Ann and said she was a social worker. Aunty Margaret explained that Ann was going to take us to two different foster families. After Mum had signed some papers, she asked that I should be placed with Shiv, and for Mina and Anju to go together. Shiv saw me as a second mother figure, and from an early age I'd learned to take care of him. Mum said he'd never settle anywhere without me, so the two of us went to one set of foster parents, while Anju and Mina were assigned to another family.

I remember being too shocked and frightened to take in what was happening, but I recall that the social worker didn't engage with us. Shankerdas refused to be put into care, running from the room declaring that at 16 he wasn't going and that he wasn't a baby. Eventually, they agreed to let him stay in the camp on his own, accepting that he was old enough to look after himself.

We had such a difficult time when we were first away from Mum. No one explained that children were expected to go to bed early, much earlier than the adults, according to our age. How my heart pined for my younger brother, who was desperate to sleep with me, but it seemed it wasn't the English way. He was forced to go to bed first, at 7 p.m.. I'd hear him sobbing himself to sleep at night. The first time I went upstairs to comfort him, stroking his head and lying next to him so he'd sleep, my foster parents scolded me severely and grounded me. For several nights, he'd pleaded me to take him to bed and my heart ached because I wasn't allowed to.

My foster mother explained I was just a child and that it was now their role as his new carers to set the rules, and I understood that – but explaining that being a second parent to him also played a role in my sense of worth was more difficult. Back in Uganda, when society saw me as someone of little worth because of my background and my illness, my parents gave me the respect and honour I deserved. Being the eldest girl in the family, they handed me the responsibility of caring for my younger brother and sisters on the days when I felt well enough. But here, it seemed things were to be different.

I later discovered that Anju and Mina were expected to kiss their foster parents goodnight – a foreign concept to us back then, this was unheard of both in Uganda and in our culture. Not only that, but Anju and Mina were also revolted at the thought of having to kiss a male.

Tears were often shed in their household when it came to daily ablutions, too. It seemed they were to be punished for washing their hair at night – their foster parents having assumed it was merely a delaying tactic to avoid going to bed. In Uganda, it was part of our culture to wash our hair every morning to prepare for the day ahead. Now, my sisters were being told to shower in the evening, so naturally they washed their hair every evening, too. This new regime was so alien; in Uganda, we'd have thought it dirty to wait until the evening to wash and it was unheard of to wash at night before bed.

In my foster home, panic ensued when my foster mother decided to take Shiv to the hairdresser one day. Thankfully, she asked me first and listened to me, so I managed to stop her. Otherwise, Mum would have been devastated, having made a vow to God that he'd only have his hair cut once she'd taken him to the Golden Temple in Amritsar, Punjab, India, after some special Sikh prayers. My foster carer clearly hadn't been told that long, natural hair was part of our Sikh faith, and fortunately she respected that, for which I was grateful.

In Uganda, we'd been used to tasty, spicy food and there was always plenty on Mum's table, but the food in the dining room in the camp and then in the foster homes was bland. Worst of all, it was rationed. We watched, disheartened, as potatoes and spoonfuls of vegetables were counted out fairly, and no one liked to ask for more.

The social worker hadn't so much as spoken a word to us, never once addressing us during visits or asking if we were okay. Given she was white and of a different background, we also assumed she wouldn't understand about any of our traditions, including that of hair-washing. Had she been Indian, she may have understood and we might have felt we could talk to her about our foster homes or ask questions. As it was, we had no relationship with her whatsoever, which was sad. We also felt we couldn't ask any questions about differences in lifestyle or culture, in case we were seen to be rude and ungrateful.

To deal with the shock of our new way of living and to comfort each other, one day we decided not to go to school and instead spend as much time together as we could in our old dormitory at the camp. We were missing being a family, the consequences far from our minds. We had no idea where Shankerdas was, though, as he was never in the dormitory when we were there, and we left Shiv with the foster parents, because he was too young to sneak away with us, although we wished he was with us, too. The other families in the camp had gone by then, so we were quite alone. We locked the door and resolved to hide under the beds in silence if anyone knocked, until the footsteps inevitably went away.

Another time, we planned to stay the night in the dormitory and hid, locking the door so it looked like it was empty. But our plan was thwarted when we heard a thunderous knocking on the door, having been missed in school. The head teacher had called home when our absence had been noticed, so it would be a double punishment coming our way now our foster carers knew.

We were ordered back to school and all of us were punished by our foster families – no one listened to our 'excuses'. We were each grounded, meaning we couldn't go out and play or watch TV – the worst punishment. We agreed privately that a few slaps would have been preferable, as at least it would have been over and done with. Grounding someone for days was more tortuous, in our opinion. It felt like no one understood our desperation to see each other.

However, that event was to be a turning point, whereby arrangements were made for our foster carers to meet up so we could all be together. My foster carers took the lead by inviting Mina and Anju to tea several times. That was very comforting to us and I considered myself lucky to have had them as foster carers. Despite the English ways – the bedtimes, the insistence that I couldn't have Shiv in bed with me or take care of him – they had very kind hearts. In their eyes, they were enabling me to be a child myself, removing the burden – after all, I was only about 12 years old.

As time went on, I was allowed to go to bed earlier, having feigned tiredness. Shiv and I struck a deal whereby he'd shut his eyes and pretend to be asleep in my bed until I came up and then I'd cuddle him until he fell asleep in my arms. Then I'd place him in his own bed and go back to mine. It was a simple comfort both he and I so desperately needed.

I knew my carers were good people, as I felt fully accepted by them, and they never shunned me when I got blisters over my body or massive ulcers in my mouth from the epidermolysis bullosa. I used to wet the bed, too, and was amazed that I was never punished for that, either. But one thing they couldn't do was help me to deal with the loneliness of being without our mum.

We started to suspect she'd died, as they'd initially told us that Mum would only be away for a few weeks, but the weeks stretched on. It felt like an eternity – and no one said a thing. No one thought to take us to see her in that first week or even during the first two months of our separation.

The social worker who came to speak to my foster carers remained invisible to me. Nothing was explained, nothing more said about Mum. My brother had whispered so many times in the night about seeing her. My carers were kind and I felt I could speak to them, trusting them to tell me the truth, so eventually I asked them outright one day if Mum had died. I was carrying my brother at the time, needing the comfort of his small body next to mine.

My foster carer tried to reassure me, but none of us had any idea what was wrong with Mum or why we'd been separated for so long. Thankfully, my foster parents took us to see her in hospital after that. They even took my sisters with us. We felt overjoyed that she was alive and tears came readily. It had been around three months since we'd last seen her and it felt like forever. So much had changed; we were happy but unhappy. Not only had my sisters got used to their carers, but Shiv and I had got used to the ways of ours, too. We had new clothes, we had warm beds and we were loved, but how we ached to be with our mum and home once more. Seeing her only deepened our desperation to be a family again.

That prayer was answered when Mum was discharged from hospital and we were reunited in the camp dormitory once more. And then another small miracle happened, when a couple of women turned up at the camp with a gift of gold. Before we'd been exiled, Mum had asked the missionaries to look after three necklace sets, so two young volunteer missionary teachers had hidden the jewellery under their clothes, in their bags and even in their books then flown to the UK to return it to Mum. This jewellery had very special worth in our family as Dad had bought each of us girls a necklace set made out of sovereigns. Because they were so ornate, Mum had decided they'd be too noticeable to wear that fateful day at the airport. I'm so grateful that our necklaces reached us in the UK. It was a little piece of Dad that both of my sisters later wore on their wedding days.

When we heard of a place called Scotland, the next round of prayers began. If Greenham Common near Newbury was cold, Scotland was said to be even colder. We were told it was a place where the sun never shone and that they spoke a different language. People like us were being sent there as it had more houses. Well, that made sense. But who wanted to live in a cold, dark place where the sun never shone?

Mum held firm. We could not, must not, go to Scotland – it was already cold enough in England, without subjecting us to further harsh temperatures. Her prayers were answered yet again. This time, the answer came in the form of a bishop in Kabale who had known Dad and had close links with the teachers at our old school. He'd contacted a Mrs Palmer, whose family had set up a milk kitchen in the camp, asking if she'd look out for us. She asked various families if they knew Dhir Engineering in Kabale, but Anju and I had never heard it, not knowing the name of the garage, as in Uganda we were known as the Chands, so it hadn't registered. But Mum said, 'Yes, that's us.'

Mrs Palmer was the patron of the Red Cross then, and she asked Anju and I if we'd like to go to Red Cross meetings to learn first aid, which is how we got to know her. When my mother told Mrs Palmer that we were soon to be sent to Scotland, she offered Shankerdas an apprenticeship. It turned out that the Palmer family owned Huntley & Palmers, the biscuit manufacturers. They had a garage for their fleet of lorries and vans, and as Shankerdas wanted to be a mechanic just like his dad, it was the perfect place for his training.

I was excited at the prospect of Shankerdas getting a job there, as I thought it would mean lots of free biscuits. But what that job actually led to was way more than that: Shankerdas' job came with a house in Berkshire near the factory, big enough for us all. That offer saved us from being subjected to Scotland, where most of the rest of the families from our camp were taken unless they had friends or relatives to arrange housing for them elsewhere. Finally, we'd be moving to a permanent home.

It seemed fated that we'd end up in Berkshire when we'd first arrived, when we could have ended up anywhere, for there I'd meet Dr Emerson, the doctor Dad was so desperate to treat me for my epidermolysis bullosa.

I'm not subscribing to the notion that it was all because of Idi Amin, or that the atrocities had had to happen in order for our family to end up in that particular part of England. It's more that we were flown to Heathrow rather than Stansted, driven to one of 16 possible camps, then ended up living a five-minute walk from the very hospital where Dr Emerson worked. It's as if my life journey and the solutions to our problems had already been mapped out.

The camps assigned to expelled Ugandans ranged from Glasgow to Blackburn, from Leicester to London. The government tried to manage the influx so we'd be placed where there was housing, although the policy didn't make much sense. For example, there was plentiful housing in Leicester and a high Asian population, but they didn't want any more of us to move there. Leicester Council even tried to curb Ugandan immigration with negative advertising campaigns warning Ugandans to stay away, but many people went regardless. People went where they needed to go, if they were able.

I'm so grateful Mum stood firm about us not being moved to Glasgow – it was so far away from the Royal Berkshire Hospital, where it seemed I was destined to be treated by Dr Emerson. Her faith always seemed to be rewarded – this time, a Divine intervention in the form of Mrs Palmer.

Coming to the UK was such a learning curve not just for us, but also for our foster carers. I'm still in touch with them to this day and, when they looked back on our time with them, they expressed much guilt. They'd received no information from social services about either our customs or our faith. All they knew was that there were a couple of children coming from Uganda. They weren't prepared for our arrival and nor were they given any formal training about what to expect.

It's so hard to understand what it means for children when they're uprooted and brought to a strange place, only to be told they have to learn to fit in with an alien culture. To their great credit, our foster carers took us in – but without the understanding that we were all traumatized. We'd been subjected to all sorts of terrors at the hands of soldiers when trying to leave Uganda, and then we'd been separated from our mother. Not only that, but we'd also just lost our father. It was no wonder that we were damaged at least in some way.

When we were older, we discovered that my mother had been admitted to hospital for a hysterectomy. However, it turned out that she'd stayed in hospital so much longer than usual because she was so depressed. She'd been through so much trauma, with five children to care for and no close relatives to call upon for support in the UK, that it was no wonder she finally crashed. We had no idea where Pritam Paaji, Dad's nephew, had gone, either, as they'd left Uganda after us. Mum felt so isolated that it's not surprising that depression set in.

Angels helped us so much via the people they brought into our lives during that time of great upheaval. There was Aunty Margaret, who was surely an angel in human disguise. She visited Mum weekly in hospital, even though she was Shiv's health visitor, and they became firm friends. After we moved from the camp to nearby Berkshire, she used to take Mum out once a week for lunch when Mum had no one to talk to. If Mum had any concerns or worries, she'd turn to Aunty Margaret.

Then we had the young volunteer teachers who had brought over our jewellery; not forgetting another missionary who'd contacted a specialist on my behalf because I was getting ulcers in my eye, which was part of my condition, who lived just a five-minute walk from our new house in Berkshire. It was he who had referred me to Dr Emerson, the renowned skin specialist, whom my dad had wanted me to see when we were back in Uganda. And of course then there was Mrs Palmer and the bishop. So many links, so much Divine intervention at work that shaped our lives from that time on.

With this change of fortune, our life in the UK could truly begin. Shankerdas had a job, so we had money coming in, and we now had a permanent home. How Mum managed to bring up five of us under such adverse conditions, I'll never know. We had so little then, but at least we had each other. And we were just so grateful to be safe.

CHAPTER 9

Mum's Challenges

After we moved in together, life returned to some form of normality. But, as soon as Mum switched on the old black-and-white TV, all hell broke loose. First of all, the TV actually worked. It had cost next to nothing at the local jumble sale, which was just as well as we only had income support to live on from week to week. We were entitled to income support because Shiv was just a couple of years old and Mum didn't speak English, so was unable to work. We were beyond excited – the only TV we'd watched had been months ago in the camp at Greenham, when we'd seen *Top of the Pops* on a Thursday evening. And even then, most of us had been banned from watching that programme again as Mum had deemed it improper – Mum, as ever, being the morality inspector. But now, we had our very own TV!

We each clamoured to watch the shows we wanted, and unfortunately we all wanted to see different TV programmes at the same time, so there was a constant battle, with each of us going up to the TV to select a different channel. It was chaos. Mum would sometimes take the indoor aerial and lock it in a cupboard just to stop the arguments. And sometimes those arguments got too much. We'd be shouting at each other, fighting over the buttons for the three channels on the TV, barely sitting down to watch anything.

Occasionally, we agreed on a programme we all liked. We'd rush home to watch a soap called *Crossroads* or our favourite crime drama, *Hawaii Five-O*. Mum would watch it with us, but as soon as a kissing scene came on she'd say disapprovingly, 'That's disgusting. Turn it over,' even turning off the TV altogether for a few minutes until she deemed it safe enough to be switched back on. By that time, sometimes we found the programme had ended altogether, as Mum's instructions to 'wait five minutes' could go on forever. I remember grumbling, 'But, Mum, no one can kiss this long, surely!'

Mum hated being the disciplinarian. That had been Dad's job. Before Dad's death, it had always been a case of 'Wait 'til your dad gets home!' One such time was when Mum found out that, yet again, we'd been caught lighting a firework and rolling it towards a car near our house. The ultimate goal was for the firework to go off under the car, so the driver would chase us. We'd be laughing hysterically as we ran back to our house via the back door – or at least we did until we heard the driver knocking furiously at the front door one day to complain to Mum.

'Wait 'til your dad gets home!' we'd chorus with glee, mimicking our exasperated mum.

We'd be jumping on our beds, chanting her words over and over. Sometimes she couldn't wait until he got home, instead picking up the phone to tell him in no uncertain terms that he had to come home right away. There would be a period of negotiation on the phone, which we'd listen in to, but Dad rarely came home until it was time to do so, by which time Mum would either have worked herself into a fury about the injustice of dealing with such miscreant children or, more optimistically on our part, she'd have forgotten about our naughty antics altogether.

Occasionally, it seemed that she'd forgotten all about it (I suspect that's what my father had hoped for, too), but then she'd suddenly remember at bedtime. By this time, Dad would have had a whiskey or two and would be in a very mellow, benevolent mood. This was good news for us, as he'd speak to Mum in a cajoling way, trying to get her to see how petty it all was. It was his belief that we were just children and that this was our time to have fun and be carefree. He felt that she should leave us be. This mood of Dad's was bad news for Mum, who could only scowl at us now that our punishment was off the agenda.

Now and again, Mum would get so frustrated with Dad's mellowness that she'd have to take on his role of disciplinarian and chase us all with a stick or her rolling pin. Sometimes when this happened, my father would whisper to us to come and hide under his blanket or in the cupboard near his armchair, then he'd direct Mum in the opposite direction when she asked if he'd seen us.

Bringing up five children alone in England was an entirely different affair, one where she had to be both our morality inspector and disciplinarian all rolled into one – both Mum and Dad, as it were.

We ran rings around her at times and I'm ashamed to say that we took advantage of her inability to read and write English. Letters would arrive, allegedly sent by the school, to say that we had a school trip and wouldn't be back until 10 or 11 p.m.. Instead, Anju and I would go and visit friends and, on one occasion, when we were 17, we went to a night club.

We only got caught when someone who could read English told Mum that school letters weren't written by hand and that they looked more official than scraps of crumpled paper produced from a school bag. The result was that Mum got stricter with us, but she did allow us to join a church youth club, as that was deemed to be a 'good, moral place'. She trusted the Christian priests to make sure we were looked after, but even they didn't escape her wrath.

She'd noticed that we'd started coming home later than her usual deadline, so she made the priest promise to escort us home by 10 p.m.. One time, the priest had had to plead with Mum to let us in the house. We were ten minutes late and she'd locked the front door, refusing to let us in. Even priests had a lot to live up to when it came to Mum's house rules.

On another occasion, Mum announced that she was leaving us after yet another row about the TV had erupted. With a strange look on her face, she'd picked up a carrier bag and marched out of the front door. We didn't take her seriously in the beginning, but after a while, when she didn't come back, we started getting anxious. There was a strange silence in the house and we didn't know what to do. It occurred to us for the first time that maybe she meant it....

Suddenly, the TV didn't matter. The programmes we'd been fighting over held no appeal. We went out into the street to look for her and laughed with joy when we found her perched on a low wall at the end of the road, her carrier bag by her side. When we approached, she started laughing, too. We promised her that we'd be good and not fight over the TV again, then we walked back home together, peace reigning once more for a few nights. That time we realized we'd gone too far and tried to be good, we really did, but soon enough, the rows began again. We were back to a sense of normality as children, being free to squabble over the slightest thing.

We soon got used to Mum's dramatic outbursts. She'd say things like 'Rip my heart out. I'm happy to die for you.' To my siblings, she'd say things like 'They had to cut my stomach open to have you and you can't even do this one thing for me?' I'd smile at this, because this was Mum all over – she could be the best drama queen ever.

It was the same when we were younger back in Uganda. When there were four of us, before my little brother Shiv was born, we'd fight at the dinner table over something simple like a chicken leg. We could all have a piece of breast, but the leg was our favourite bit and we'd squabble over a chicken curry every time. Mum would extend her legs and say, 'Would you like me to chop one off so you can all have a piece of leg?' Or she'd sigh and throw her hands up in the air then say, 'Where am I going to get a four-legged chicken, that's what I'd like to know?'

The most dramatic moment came, however, when Mum lay on the road in front of a bus. She'd left the house in exasperation after yet another squabble had begun over the TV.

'What *are* you doing, Mum?' I cried when we saw the commotion outside from our living room window and ran out to investigate.

'I'm asking the bus driver to run me over and put me out of my misery,' Mum replied, ever so calmly and with as much dignity as a woman lying prostrate on tarmac could muster.

The driver marched up to us, glaring, and berated us for our behaviour. We were very ashamed indeed, but the months that followed were blissfully peaceful, as we left the TV to Shankerdas and instead played board games we'd bought from a jumble sale.

Mum's frustration with our behaviour never stopped her from being compassionate, though. It was just in her nature – she never held a grudge or stopped trying to help others.

One day, an aunt of mine came to see Mum. It was the same aunty who'd lived in Kampala and who'd turned Dad and me away when we'd asked to stay with them before my treatment at Mulago Hospital. She'd left Uganda, too, and now lived in the Midlands. She'd travelled to see Mum in Berkshire not just for a family visit, but for what turned out to be some serious advice.

The minute I saw her on our doorstep, I knew why she'd come. Weeping, she'd pointed to her daughter, who was covered from head to toe in eczema. She'd heard from other relatives that my skin had improved and that I'd been seeing this amazing specialist called Dr Emerson at the Royal Berkshire Hospital. Mum gave her all the support she needed. She could easily have turned her away, but she didn't let the past dictate the present or the future. Instead, she welcomed my aunty into our home and let them stay with us in Berkshire whenever they had an appointment with the specialist. She was now on the same quest for a cure or treatment that my parents had been on all those years ago, bringing us together through our mutual pain.

My cousin's eczema had undoubtedly been triggered by the stress of leaving Uganda, but my aunt chose to blame it on karma. It was only when I was much older that I realized what she meant by karma – what goes around, comes around. Rather than dwell on the karmic lesson my aunt chose to see in her daughter's eczema, I now see the true karma in my mother's ability to forgive. She'd sheltered that family in the past and then, despite my aunt's rejection of me, she still helped her. She simply saw a mother who desperately wanted a cure for her daughter. And Mum could certainly relate to that.

~

CHAPTER 10

Cinzano Days

One day, we'd sneaked off during school lunchbreak to go to Lindsey's house – a friend of my best friend, Donna. It was here I had my first taste of alcohol, and I remember feeling very important and grown-up when she'd handed me the drink.

'Try it,' she'd encouraged invitingly. 'It's delicious.'

I was nervous in case it made me drunk, but she assured me it was too weak for that. Instead, she believed it would certainly make me feel good, so I took a tentative sip, expecting to grimace or throw up. I'd once sneaked a sip of my dad's whiskey when he wasn't looking and remembered how disgusting the taste was. To my astonishment, this potion was most delicious. I discovered it was called Cinzano and it appeared her parents were fine with the fact she was drinking.

I was fascinated. I'd never have dared do something like this at home. At 15, I was forbidden from leaving the school grounds at lunchtime, never mind from touching alcohol.

We all looked up to Lindsey. She was a commanding presence who challenged authority and her parents took no nonsense from anyone, either – something we'd never have dared to do. One day, her mother came up to the school and physically slapped a teacher for putting Lindsey in detention. We were actually all in detention at the time because of another child's wrongdoing – if one of us misbehaved, the whole class was punished – and that day, we were rescued by Lindsey's mother, so we were in awe, even if it did mean her being banned from the school premises after that for her actions.

The chants the bullies invariably greeted me with as they announced my arrival at school every morning made me grateful for *any* offer of friendship, so when my best and only friend, Donna, asked me to join her in this secret adventure out of school, I was only too happy to oblige. I was glad to have someone at least taking an interest in me and so, despite my worries about letting down the teachers and getting caught, I went anyway. I was so desperate to be liked by more than one person that it was worth the risk.

Lindsey informed me that her parents knew she drank and that they didn't mind. Her brother chose that moment to walk into the room and he was adamant that we shouldn't get drunk. I remember thinking how good-looking he was and Lindsey said that all the girls were after him. She said this in a very matter of fact way – just like that, taken for granted. So I sipped my Cinzano and lemonade, savouring the taste. Not wanting us to get done in school by showing up drunk, she'd warned us not to drink it in one go and to take sips.

I was horrified at the prospect of getting expelled, because I knew that was the penalty if you were found drunk in school – it had already happened with some girls. But it was too late now. I'd already taken a sip and I loved it.

This will be my drink when I'm older, I resolved. *This will be my grown-up drink.*

I felt light-headed when we left for school.

'Shh – don't breathe a word to anyone,' Lindsey said sternly when we slipped through the school gates. 'No one must know.'

We nodded solemnly, already anticipating another excursion to Cinzano-and-lemonade heaven. The afternoon passed in a pleasant haze!

Don't ask me what I was taught that day. All I remember is feeling very mellow and that life was indeed good.

These furtive excursions continued. We'd invariably see Lindsey's brother and he'd smile knowingly when we arrived. On one occasion he sat with us, which made Donna and me very giggly and feel even more adult that he took an interest in us. Then came the revelation!

As we walked back to school one day, Lindsey told Donna that her brother felt it was a shame she was coloured, because he said she was actually really pretty and that he'd fancy her if she were white. Donna looked pleased that he at least fancied her, even though her skin was the wrong colour. Then Lindsey turned to me, seemingly entertained by what he said about me, for some reason: as she imparted that he felt it was a shame I had a face like a chewed-up toffee. I stared at Lindsey and tried to comprehend what she was saying. My brain felt befuddled. I'd had a glass and a half of Cinzano and lemonade, but I remember wishing I hadn't, as I was feeling distinctly sick and dizzy. I knew it had been a mistake to drink more than one glass. *Was it the drinks or the words?*

The school bell went then and we ambled off to our lessons. But I couldn't concentrate – the words kept repeating themselves over and over. *A face like a chewed-up toffee. A face like a chewed-up toffee.* I surreptitiously touched my face. I tried to feel the contours with my fingers to try to work out where it looked chewed up. *Which part of my face had he referred to?*

That night, I stood before a mirror, examining my skin: I still had scars from the blisters I'd had from my epidermolysis bullosa. Suddenly, all I could think was how my parents had lied to me when they'd said I was pretty. How my friends had lied to me when they'd said I was beautiful.

I stared in the mirror, right into my soul. *Wow! How had I not seen it?* He was right – I did have a face like a chewed-up toffee. I felt sad that no one had told me. Her brother was right – I was ugly. And I knew from that moment on that I was never going to believe anyone who told me I was pretty.

How I wished at the time that those words would go away, that they'd never been voiced, but as it was, they haunted me day and night. Each time I asked Mum if I was pretty, she'd respond that I was beautiful. And each time I'd tearfully fling those words right back at her, telling her she was only saying that because she was my mother. Then I'd beg her to stop lying to me.

Genuine compliments did come later when Donna told me her cousin really fancied me and that he thought I was beautiful, which was exactly what I wanted to hear as a despairing teenager. Sometimes I'd hear voices in my dreams that I was loved and that I was pretty. But the harsh memories of being told I had a 'face like a chewed-up toffee' drowned out those voices.

I now know words are powerful. Words can cut. And their impact can last a lifetime. It's so true when they say the tongue is sharper than the sword. A cut from a sword will heal in time, but words that are spoken can deeply influence a person's thoughts, their sense of worth and their actions forever.

I never went back to that so-called friend's house and, years later, I still think of that incident. It left me with an odd love for Cinzano and lemonade – I do enjoy the occasional tipple – but otherwise I spent years agonizing over that young man's words, replaying the humiliation. Sometimes I'd want to curl up in a ball and never leave the house again. It affected me to the point where I couldn't even look people in the face. The first thing I thought when I met anybody was *I've got a face like a chewed-up toffee. Now they'll know how ugly I am.*

Eventually, when I couldn't torture myself any longer, I allowed my worth to speak. I thought to myself, *Do you know what? He isn't lying in bed ten years later thinking about what he said to me. Why am I being consumed by the opinions of people who really don't hold much significance in my life? Why am I letting their views dictate my life? Why am I giving them power?* No. I needed to take that power back, to be absolutely clear that, from now on, others' perceived opinions wouldn't affect me.

I realized it didn't matter how people judged my face, my colour, or who they thought I was or should be. What was more important was how I felt inside. I recognized that the only person continually hurting myself was me, so surely the only person who could stop that hurt was also me. What I didn't know then was that I'd have to learn that lesson more than once.

Someone who I deemed my protector during my school years, aside from my lovely sister Anju, was Donna. Having Donna as my best friend in school was such a blessing. She was like a sister to me during my secondary-school years and she stuck with me throughout all the bullying. She really helped me to build my sense of self-worth and she never once let me down. We'd walk to and from school together and spend hours chatting away after school in one another's houses. She showed me how to use moisturizer on my skin and plait my hair – those things teenage girls love doing together. Her family totally accepted me without question, never commenting on my scars and blisters, and I felt welcomed by the warm hug her mum always gave me when I entered their home. I visited as often as I could and was always invited to stay for the family meal. Whenever I ate her food, she had a habit of saying 'Ah so,' with a satisfied smile, for she loved it when people enjoyed her food and showed their appreciation by asking for more. Their acceptance of my presence was balm to my bruised soul. But the fact remained that my schooldays were never easy.

As a teenager, I'd confide in Mum about how terrible I felt about myself – I was lucky to have a parent I could actually say that to

– and she'd do everything she could to try to make me feel better about myself. But I was becoming immune to her encouragement – and to any other positive feedback I got, for that matter. I'd even interpret a compliment as criticism, just in case a conversation-opener was a trick. If someone said I looked nice in a sari, I'd refute their claims and tell them I looked fat. If they said I looked really well, I'd say, 'You mean I don't look ugly today!' I overanalysed whatever anyone said to me and made my own mind up about how I really thought they looked at me. I even had periods during which I felt suicidal. The bullying at school was never-ending and my self-loathing became so painful emotionally that I wanted to die.

Once, I'm ashamed to say, I even voiced my opinion to Mum. 'I wish I was dead. I just want to kill myself,' I said.

'Why would you want to do that,' she retorted, 'when your father risked his life to save you?'

She then told me a story about my past that was, and still is, very disturbing. She did it to shock me back to reality, so I could see that my life really was worth fighting for.

Apparently, when I was around 18 months old, my parents took us to see my grandparents in India. We set sail from Mombasa, Kenya, destined for the city of Bombay – now Mumbai – to begin a trip that was to last six months. We were to visit my father's parents in Jalandhar, Punjab and then go on to Hoshiarpur, also in Punjab, to stay with my maternal grandparents.

We boarded the ship for the eight- to ten-day journey, but given what occurred on the voyage, for my parents it would have felt like an interminable length of time, for a fellow passenger tried to drown me. For my safety, the staff were forced to keep both us and the assailant separate from one another thereafter, so we took to sleeping on the deck. Strangely enough, my mother and Shankerdas still managed to recall the positives: the fact that we had our own space away from the crowds below deck and that the nights were beautiful. Unlike the others, at least we could feel the cool breeze and gaze at the stars shimmering in the night sky.

The man in question had violently tried throw me overboard, believing I was causing them a sense of humiliation or shame. Mum was holding me, and apparently he grabbed me from her arms, shouting, 'Let me save you from your dishonour!' Having decided just by looking at me that I was the result of an affair that my mother or father must have had with an African, he believed he was surely doing my parents a favour.

Shocked, Mum tried to wrestle me from his grip and screamed for my dad to help. At the time, he was at the other end of the boat, but when he heard her screams, he came running. Dad punched my attacker on sight and placed me in the safety of my mother's arms once again. As they fought, the man continued to shout that my parents had brought a scandal and sense of disgrace to our family. The sight of me affronted him so much that he felt he had the right to drown me, thereby saving both of my parents from having their reputation tarnished.

Why this man felt he had the right to do this, I'll never know. How he could pick up someone else's child and say he didn't like the look of it, that he was just going to kill it for them, and that they'd thank him later, was beyond me. But the fact remained that Dad had saved me – he'd been willing to die for me. It also made me question whether or not I'd have survived had Dad not been there. I think not. I truly believe that I'd have been thrown overboard had he not intervened.

This man evidently thought he was God – the one from the Old Testament who I'd been brought up with and who had ultimate control over our lives. Mum's story was devastating to hear the first time, because it chimed with the comments and the prejudices I'd endured throughout my life. But then I saw what Mum wanted me to see when I was in the depths of my depression following the bullying: that I was worth something. I may have held little worth for some people in the community, but the worth I held in my parents' eyes was tangible. And it was an important memory for both Mum and me of my father, who was no longer with us, making us remember Dad for his strength and commitment to us all.

~

CHAPTER 11

A Message from Above

When Mum eventually got to meet Dr Emerson, he enquired of her as to whether or not my condition was genetic and whether anyone else in the family suffered from epidermolysis bullosa. Mum requested that I leave the room before she'd reply, but I knew exactly what she was going to tell him, so I saved her the bother of explaining, and turned and said, 'I'm adopted, Mum. I know I'm adopted – have done for years. There's no need for secrets now.'

I can almost hear the static crackle in the air even now, reminding me of Dad trying to tune in our old radio back in Uganda. It felt like I was pushing through the charged air as I persisted. I looked at Dr Emerson and repeated, 'I'm adopted. They know nothing about my family history. I'm sorry we can't help. We have no idea who they are.'

This was the first time Mum and I had ever openly acknowledged my adoption. I was fifteen years old and it had taken a crisis for it to happen.

I'd woken that morning with flu-like symptoms, as if I had a terrible cold. Strangely, my nose wasn't blocked or streaming, but I had a raging fever and my joints ached horribly – even lifting my limbs was an effort. I was covered in blisters from head to toe and a painful rash had appeared on my face. It was normal for me to have blisters coming and going, but now I had full-blown blisters just about everywhere on my body.

I put all of my new symptoms down to a flare-up of epidermolysis bullosa. I knew that stress was a factor and I'd certainly been feeling under lots of pressure, what with the incessant bullying at school, not to mention the continuous shame I felt about my appearance. Another theory both Dr Emerson, and Dr Desai in Uganda, had put forwards was that my blisters could be down to an allergic reaction to the sun's ultraviolet rays. It was the summer of 1976 and we were in the middle of a heatwave at the time, so that certainly might have explained it. Not only that, but the heat that day felt unbearable, which would have exacerbated the condition. The final possibility was that my disease was genetic, which was impossible to determine, given that no one knew my history.

The only thing we could be sure of was that my skin disorder wasn't just serious, but also incredibly rare. Back then, Dr Emerson had told us there were just ten known sufferers in the world. However, I was about to discover that my illness that day was something even more life-threatening than epidermolysis bullosa.

It seemed fortuitous that I had an appointment to see Dr Emerson, the skin consultant, that morning about the blisters. I could barely get out of bed, but at least he'd be able to see how bad it was for himself. However, he was more interested in the rash on my face than all the blisters. His expression was grave when he told Mum how ill I really was. He believed I had a condition called systemic lupus erythematosus, so he arranged for me to be admitted to hospital immediately for tests.

I felt no sense of alarm, just curiosity at what it would be like in a hospital in England. My first thought was that I'd be able to lie down all day without having to help around the house. Then I wondered if I'd get pinched by various doctors to see if my skin would blister, like I'd had to endure in Uganda. That thought quelled my curiosity and I began to feel anxious. Mum had started weeping by now, so I knew I had to push my own anxieties aside and be strong for her. It really didn't register with me how serious this new diagnosis, along with my epidermolysis, really was.

'It's okay,' I soothed. 'I'll be fine, Mum. You'll see. They'll look after me. They always do.'

I don't remember the ride to the hospital much. I think by the time the ambulance got me there, I was too tired to care. The next thing I knew, I was being pushed down the corridor in a wheelchair. The porter was wheeling me fast and I felt a gentle breeze around my hot, sore cheeks. Every now and then I glimpsed yet another person looking at me with what I took to be a mixture of curiosity, sympathy and revulsion. I felt embarrassed and hung my head so no one could see me.

I lay in my hospital bed with fans whirring to keep me cool. I'd be shivering one minute then scalding hot the next, but I remember feeling grateful for the soft, cocooning sheets that made me feel safe and cared for. I heard tiny voices from afar say how hot I was – unbearably hot. The nurses would come and go, taking skin samples for their biopsies.

I was given a very high dose of the steroid prednisone, which I'd first taken in tiny amounts as a child in Uganda, but at fifteen I was now given an adult dose. Dr Emerson also prescribed baths in potassium permanganate to toughen my fragile skin. I took those baths every day, where I was lowered into water that had turned a deep purple owing to the permanganate. The baths seemed to soothe my skin at first, but then I started to stick to the bathtub. When the nurses lifted me out of the water, the skin on my thighs and bottom came away and wouldn't heal. The doctor stopped the baths, but I continued to take the steroids, along with immunosuppressants for the lupus. The staff did everything they could to help me and although they couldn't cure me, they could at least alleviate the pain.

I felt so distant from everything and everyone. All I wanted was the incessant aching in my joints to cease. Sometimes I'd touch my face and it would feel wet – no tears, just pus or blood from the rash. Then one day I caught a glimpse of my face in a mirror. It wasn't me! *Not me!* I couldn't stop shaking as I stared in fascinated horror at what I'd become. The sores on my cheek made me recoil. My thick, curly locks of hair were all but gone. All I had now were tufts, as I had so many blisters on my scalp. I was so bloated because of the steroids that my face had swelled into a huge moon. I was officially a monster!

I remember looking up to the ceiling thinking, *What else are you going to throw at me, God?* I wasn't sure how much more could I take. My cries of pain and disbelief brought a nurse and the ward sister to my bed. They tried to console me, but how do you comfort the inconsolable? After all, there was nothing they could say that would make me believe I'd ever get my looks back again. The sister ordered that all mirrors be taken out of the room. I lay on my side, pulled up the covers and hid from the world.

'I'm an ugly duckling – that's what I am,' I'd mournfully say to myself.

But then, maybe I'd never been a swan. Maybe I'd been kidding myself all along – *a swan, indeed.*

At some point, the stress and tiredness must have been too much for my mum. She was getting up early, shopping and cooking, and then visiting me at Battle Hospital in Berkshire, which was a 20-minute bus ride away. Occasionally she'd walk to the hospital, which would take over an hour. She'd spend the whole afternoon with me and leave when visiting hours were over. Anju was entrusted with looking after Shiv and Mina, feeding both them and Shankerdas when he returned from work.

Then one day, Mum collapsed. She was diabetic and hadn't been monitoring her sugar levels. We ended up on the same ward – Mum on one side in her bed and me on the other in mine. She was discharged after two weeks. Selfishly, I felt bereft of her company.

Being ill had made me come to appreciate Mum more than ever. She gave me her company and her time, and she cared for me implicitly, but it had made me greedy for more of her time. I'm ashamed to admit that I had tantrums if she couldn't visit me at times because she needed to rest at home. I could never expect to grow emotionally, knowing that I was forcing Mum to attend to my needs at the expense of the rest of her children at home. I knew I was being selfish by insisting she stay with me, and that made me feel worse rather than better. To allow myself to grow spiritually in worth, I had to be prepared to share her with my brothers and sisters. And Mum had to rest, to look after her own needs. After all, how could she help me if she was already bent double?

Then came the day when I lapsed into unconsciousness. It was an innocent mistake on the part of the hospital, really. I wanted to sleep and, hey presto, along came the nurses with the medicine trolley. They asked if anyone wanted a sleeping tablet and I said, 'Yes, I want one, please.' I couldn't wait to be free of pain, even just for a few hours.

I fell into a deep sleep. The sweetest, most comfortable sleep ever.

From far away, I remember hearing voices.

'Bharti – can you hear me? Wake up. Come on, it's breakfast time. Aren't you hungry?'

I wanted to open my eyes, but it seemed impossible. I was deep in the soft cotton of my bed, far away in my own little world, in which only vague voices drifted in and out. It seemed I'd overdosed – they'd given me too much. I was floating above, looking down below at my own body lying there – bloated, eyes firmly shut. I felt doctors trying to prise open my eyes, saw them looking into my pupils with mini torches. I heard urgent whispers and frantic discussions, their faces grave.

I wanted to shout, 'Hey! Look at me. I'm okay. I can see you. I can hear you. I'm fine.'

I could hear everything that was going on, but I couldn't actually react. It was how I'd imagined an out-of-body experience in which I could see and hear people, but I couldn't respond.

It was that sleeping tablet that may have been the trigger for the coma I was about to slip into, which I was later told was to last for around two weeks. The doctors were deeply concerned at my extreme reaction to the sleeping tablets and were convinced that I'd gone into a comatose state because of the lupus. They believed my autoimmune cells were attacking my inner organs, mistaking them for an infection. They said I wouldn't regain consciousness and that the lupus, which had already attacked my kidneys, would kill me.

But I wasn't dead to the world: I could sense Mum's presence around me every day. She'd be touching my hair and I could hear the doctors saying, 'I'm sorry, there's not much we can do for her, Mrs Dhir.'

The consultant's words were far worse, though.

'All you have left now is prayer. She doesn't have much time.'

I felt Mum gently pat my tufts of hair with a warm towel.

'You *will* get better,' she murmured. 'If you truly love me, you will get better. Now, it's up to you. Do you think I brought you here to die? If you die, you'll break my heart and then I'll die, too. Do you want your brothers and sisters to be left without a mum?'

She was giving me the complete Indian-mum guilt trip – and it was on full power. She'd do anything to make me better, as I was to discover.

Later that week, apparently, Mum and Anju took a detour to an agricultural show on their way to visit me in hospital. It wasn't something my mother would normally have chosen to do, but that day she felt compelled to go into the field to see the show. While she was walking around, she felt a great shroud of despair enveloping her and began to feel light-headed and faint, so Mum and Anju stopped to rest on a bench.

Mum was staring into space, not at anything or anyone in particular, when a traveller woman approached her. Expecting her to be selling something like heather in exchange for luck, my mother started to open her purse to buy whatever she was offering, but the woman stopped her.

'No, I don't want anything,' she said. 'I've come with a message. You have a daughter who's very ill and the doctors have given up hope. I've come to tell you that there is hope.' Then she looked at my mum with a gaze so piercing that Mum said she felt she was looking into the depths of her soul. 'Do you have faith?' the woman asked.

Mum nodded vigorously.

'At exactly midnight tonight, take a raw egg and bury it in your garden. I will say a prayer at exactly the same time. All will be well. The illness won't leave her, but it'll never be this severe again. You'll never again have to worry about her health or fear that she's going to die.'

The woman smiled, turned on her heels and disappeared, leaving my Mum stunned. My sister was terrified. She'd never liked anything out of the norm and was desperate to leave.

Much to my sister's horror, Mum did exactly as she was told and buried an egg in the front garden at midnight as instructed. Anju, however, was appalled at the very thought of it and begged her not to do it, believing it all to be nothing but black magic. Mum did it anyway, believing she had nothing to lose.

That same night, I woke with a start. I'd just had a dream in which I'd heard the strongest voice. I didn't see anything in the dream – no shapes, no colour – I simply heard a clear voice in the darkness. And that voice said to me, 'You're going to be fine. You're going to live and you're going to help people.'

I sensed a bright light behind my eyes. I don't know if one of the nurses had come to my bedside with a torch, but I'm sure I'd have remembered if that were the case. I personally believe that the being with the voice was in that light. And it was a very kind, calm and steady voice. It was as if the firmness in that voice was communicating my need for faith, as if it were saying: 'You have to believe you're going to live.'

I didn't recognize the speaker. The voice was male, and at first I questioned if it had been my dad in spirit, because it was so comforting to me. Perhaps Dad had become my spirit guide. Whatever it was, the voice felt heaven-sent and the message for me was crystal clear: 'Stop shunning your life.' It was then that I knew I had to conquer my self-rejection, to believe that I was meant to survive.

The very next morning, Mum got a phone call from the hospital informing her that I was awake. When I came round, I remember my body feeling heavy, but a gnawing hunger in my belly had me opening my eyes and trying to sit up. I felt light-headed. It was then that I came to love hospital porridge. To be honest, I've never tasted porridge like it – sweet nectar!

I wondered why the nurse looked so shocked. By all accounts, she'd been wishing me 'Good morning' for days on end without any expectation of a response, only that day was different. I remember looking at her, puzzled. *Of course I was awake! It was morning and time for breakfast....*

A huge smile crossed her face and she went running from the ward to fetch the sister. My room flooded with doctors and nurses after that, all vying with each other to get a look at me.

One doctor took my hand. 'Well now, you gave us quite a scare,' he said.

I was baffled and couldn't understand what all the fuss was about.

'You've been out cold for a long time,' he explained.

'Really?' I asked. 'How long?'

'Two weeks,' came the reply.

And there I was thinking I'd only slept for one night.

In total, I spent nearly six months in hospital to recover fully. My finger joints had locked, so I couldn't hold a spoon to feed myself, and when I first tried to get out of bed, I had no strength whatsoever, my muscles having atrophied. The doctors explained that this meant that they'd wasted away through lack of use, meaning that I needed help to stand and walk. I also had painful bedsores and blisters from the friction when I was being turned. But I was alive.

I now know angels come in different guises. They come and they go at times when they're needed. For several years after, my mum went to the agricultural show. She wanted to thank the woman, but she never saw her again.

The angel's mission had been accomplished.

———

Later, when I was at home recovering, Mum and I revisited the adoption conversation where we'd left off when I was admitted to hospital. She asked how I knew and how long I'd known, so I told her about the file I'd read with my name on it in Dad's study. It was then that she told me the story of Goddess Lakshmi and her message that Mum had to find me and adopt me – even though she was seven months' pregnant with Anju at the time.

Mum was incredibly spiritual and she held huge faith in the Divine. She followed the Sikh religion and she also believed in the power of Hindu deities too, having been exposed to Hinduism as a child growing up in India and then as a married woman in Kabale, where the Indian population was mainly Hindu. Both in Uganda and in the UK, Sikh *shabads* (hymns) were played in our homes. There was only one Hindu temple in Kabale and we attended prayer ceremonies there as a family. Both Sikh and Hindu religious events were held either in each other's homes or at the temple.

Mum had listened to the goddess in her dreams and, against all the odds, and all the prejudice from others against a mixed-heritage child like me, I'd become her daughter. And when she'd needed to have faith that I wouldn't die, a message came from the traveller woman. Then I'd heard that voice in the night telling me not to give up and to accept myself. Coincidences? Belief? You decide. For me, it was Divine intervention.

The morning I woke up in the hospital, I felt such conviction that I wasn't destined to die from either the epidermolysis bullosa or the lupus, as some of the healers and priests had foretold. My other near-death experiences began to make sense, too: I wasn't meant to perish from dehydration, or hunger, or fall prey to animals when I'd been abandoned as a baby. I wasn't meant to die from a soldier's gunshot in Uganda. My near-death experience in hospital gave me real faith in myself and it got me thinking, *Yes, I may have these illnesses, and sometimes I may feel bad, but do you know what? I'm not going to die, because that's not my destiny. My destiny is not to come all this way in the world and die – at least, not yet, not now.*

I now sense that my destiny is to help others, not only in general, but also those suffering from lupus and epidermolysis bullosa. I feel that I've been put on this Earth to explain to them that there *is* something out there for them. My worth said that these experiences would enable me to reach out to somebody else – and I fully intended to do so.

I often think of those four events and I now know that those messages were there to guide both Mum and myself so that we'd meet each other and stay together as mother and daughter in this lifetime. For me, the story of Goddess Lakshmi, the message from the traveller at the agricultural show and the voice in the darkness proved to me that it doesn't matter what faith you are. When a message is important, it'll find you. You'll hear the truth you need at the relevant time. Mum was Sikh, the traveller was Romany and my spirituality is nothing you could label, but I've always had a sense of guidance around me.

When I was finally well enough to return to school, I discovered that everyone had been talking about me. Would you believe – they thought I'd been in hospital because I had cancer.... Then, as my absence stretched from a few weeks to six months, the next rumour was that I'd died. Barely anyone knew me at school, yet they'd drawn their own conclusions from the sight of my constantly sore, blistering skin, with no foundation for their theories. But then, I suppose the rumours of my demise did bring about a surprise bonus, for when I returned to school, even the bullies came up to me and said how sorry they were for what they'd put me through. And the best part – no one ever bullied me after that.

~

CHAPTER 12

The Power of Words

In my bedroom in our student house in Hull, I stared at myself in the mirror. I could scarcely believe what I'd done to myself. I was fixated on a small speck of blood on the corner of my lip

I'd been washing my hair while the other girls were out. I was always careful not to let them see me without my headscarf, as years of epidermolysis bullosa had taken some of my hair, leaving me with bald patches, and I felt very sensitive about anyone noticing. The last thing I wanted was for friendships to be impacted or for it to lead to bullying once more, having left that all behind. However, on this particular day, one of the girls came back earlier than expected and caught me without my scarf, freshly washed tufts of hair exposing the damage the disease had done. Then she did the very thing I'd been dreading.

'You look like a half-plucked chicken!' she laughed, pointing.

I turned it into a joke, clucking at her and grinning and laughing along, but her description really hurt. As soon as I could, I slipped away to my bedroom, to be met by a wave of anger and self-pity. I looked at myself in the mirror and physically punched my cheek as hard as I could. I wanted to scream in pain, but that would have drawn attention, so I contented myself by shouting at God in my mind. Those hateful words came back again to haunt me: 'You have a face like a chewed-up toffee.'

'Why did You make me? Did it make You happy to make me look like this?' I asked of God.

I hated myself so much. For me, at that time, everything about me spelled 'ugly'. Nothing about me felt good or right. My worth was tied up in that mocking laughter, which I could still hear as I stood before the mirror. I remembered all the words that had taunted me throughout my life and I felt like the labels were never going to leave me. So, just for good measure, in case God hadn't realized the extent of my torment, I punched myself again. This time, I split my lip and a trickle of blood ran down my chin. I wondered how on earth I was going to explain that....

My skin stung and I had a throbbing pain in my cheek. The story Mum had told me about Dad rescuing me on the boat when I was a baby had all but disappeared in that moment – the value of my self-worth impressed on me by my father gone in an instant. At 18, as I'd packed up my belongings to go away to Hull University, I'd decided to impress that story on my memory and take it with me. I could then recall it whenever I needed to feel Dad around me, to give me a sort of anchor, because at that time I had such a distorted sense of self. But it wasn't enough to stop me from sinking now.

A sense of panic washed over me. What if I bruised? How would I explain that? Worse still: what if the Christians I'd met at university found out? I knew some of them seemed to get revelations about their friends' state of faith, finances or relationships during prayer time, so it was entirely possible they'd instinctively know the real reason. I was so afraid of being exposed as someone who was questioning God; of being seen for what I then felt: a fraud!

I sat on the edge of my bed dabbing my lip with a tissue, dreading being discovered for what I was. How I must have hated myself to do that.... I was ashamed. In that moment, I was in a deep pit of despair. I couldn't face anyone and didn't leave my room that evening. I curled into a ball, pulled up the bed covers and went to sleep. Nor did I say a prayer. To me, there was nothing more to be said. But I couldn't go on like this – that much I knew.

That night, I dreamed that someone had entered my room. In my dream, I felt a weight on my bed, and I woke with a start. My heart pounding with fear, I looked around, but there was nothing there. Yet, I still sensed someone sitting on the edge of my bed. Half asleep and half awake, I fell into what seemed a kaleidoscope of images. I saw all the times I'd been hurt by a remark about my colour, my heritage, my looks, my hair. Next, I heard once more all the hateful things that had been said as I relived my horror. Then another image appeared – one of all of those people sleeping peacefully in their beds, not a care on their faces. But in the meantime, there was me – tossing, turning and shrinking from the world, not comfortable with being seen by anyone.

I felt a deep sense of shame and knew it was time to change my perception of myself. It was either that or go back home to

Berkshire and lock myself away from the world for good. The latter wasn't an option, for I realized I did love life. I wanted to live life without having to worry about other people and what they thought of me. I'd spent years agonizing over what strangers – as that's what they were, in reality – thought of me. I'd let their words affect my worth to the point where I saw nothing worthy about myself. I'd grown up surrounded by both Eastern and Western ideas of beauty, finding myself wanting in all areas over and over.

I made a vow there and then – I was never going to hurt myself again, or give people the power to bring me down. With this in mind, my worth could only grow from here. I was so much more than such a shallow thing as looks. I decided to take control by deciding that those hurtful words would no longer control me – I'd no longer give them power.

I sat up and wrote down all the words that I'd allowed to torture me, reducing my worth, for so many years. As I wrote them down, I whispered, 'You have no power over me. Go away!' I held the sheet of paper out of my window and kept repeating this mantra until it fluttered out of my hand as I released it – in my imagination, I was handing it over to God. I felt such a sense of release, bringing about relief. I turned towards the 'being' on my bed, no longer afraid. Instead, I felt comforted. It was then that I opened my eyes and realized I'd had a very powerful dream. That being who came to me in the night may well have been my guardian angel or my dad's spirit, and over time the memory of it has faded – but the lesson I received, of self-worth, will always remain with me.

Looking back, I believe I hit such a low point because of all the accumulated criticisms and name-calling I'd endured up until that point. I'd heard them so often that I'd come to believe them. But in reality, they were merely others' unfounded judgments. Yet, it's these words that I've carried with me on my life journey, which I now choose to release, for they mean nothing – they're not my truth. Now, I have a new truth.... They were like a slow poison, dripping into my mind and infecting both my physical and emotional wellbeing. It is these that I now share with you here:

'Her mother slept with a black man.'

'Her father slept with a black woman.'

'What an honourable man her father is for allowing that girl into the family and treating her like his own.'

'What an honourable woman her mother is for allowing her husband's infidelity and that girl into the family.'

'Here comes a black monkey. Look out for her – she's come in this shop to steal.'

'Don't let her touch your baby – her illness may be catching.'

'If you had to adopt, why not a boy? Not only have you got a girl, but she's black and not even pretty. Who is going to marry her?'

'She's black – the bringer of bad luck.'

This last insult being somewhat ironic, given I was thought of as such a 'lucky child'. Things were no different when we first came to England, either, where on seeing me, people praised Mum, believing she'd brought her servant over from Uganda. When Mum told them that I was her daughter, they told her that God would bless her for bringing up a servant as her own daughter. But still she'd protest I was hers, not a servant. For whatever reason, people just couldn't conceive that my parents had adopted me. My sister and I used to laugh about it, but Mum would get really riled.

For young girls going into arranged marriages in the 1970s, offensive comments were bandied about among relatives in the hope their future husband wouldn't turn out to be black or dark. They were completely oblivious to my feelings. I wondered what colour they thought I was when I was stood right in front of them and how they thought such words weren't offensive to me when they said them in my presence. When a baby was born, they'd say that they'd added to their bloodline, for it was believed that only a true member of the family could have their blood. If they'd realized what those words meant to an adopted child who knew she wasn't of their blood, would they still have said them? Would they have believed the same then?

Anju's full name is Niranjana, but when we first went to school in the UK, the head teacher renamed her as she struggled to pronounce Niranjana, so she decided to make it simpler for everyone. Her nickname when with family was Anju, but in her wisdom, the head thought she should be called Angela. I was actually somewhat jealous of this, the head deeming my two-syllable name acceptable. However, she pronounced it 'Bar-ty' to rhyme with 'farty', which of course became a great source of amusement to the other children and a torment to me. 'Here comes Farty Barty!' they'd say. I'd have done anything to be called Angela. In fact, when I was 15, I announced to Mum that I'd decided to change my name by deed poll to Barbara.

'Barbara? *Barbara?* What kind of name is Barbara?' she said.

'It's an English name and it's a very nice name, Mummyji.'

In reality, I didn't actually want to be called Barbara, so what possessed me to come up with that one is anyone's guess. But at the time, it was the only name I could think of that began with a B. I started laughing through my tears at the absurdity of it. I knew how ridiculous I sounded, but still I persisted, if only not to be called Farty Barty.

'But we've given you a really lovely name,' Mum protested. 'Why on earth would you want to change it?'

Every day, I tormented Mum in the belief that if I became Barbara, all would be good in my world. Now, I realize it was because I felt the need to project a certain image, or to say or do things, just to fit in and not lose friends. But when we do that, we're accepting others' definition of our value rather than our own.

People who know your worth accept you just as you are. If you have to change anything about yourself to get others to love you, then you're denying your sense of worth, thereby crushing the strength that comes from self-belief and self-love. Would I have been any happier if my name had changed to Barbara? I doubt it. I like my name, Bharti, but at the time, other people's distortions had made me come to hate it. I only stopped needling my poor mother when she turned to me one day with tears in her eyes and told me of how she came to name me.

She explained how the name Bharti was given to me with such love and pride by Mrs Chandarana, who was a Gujarati Hindu. My father respected both her and her husband, my Uncleji, immensely, as they'd shown him much love and acceptance when he first moved to Kabale, to the extent that he declared her his sister. We grew up calling her *Bhuaji* – 'aunty'(father's sister) – and considered her children to be our cousins.

My parents lost seven children before we were born, as a result of Mum's diabetes. Bhuaji prayed for my mum to have a healthy child and Mum fell pregnant with Shankerdas. Thereafter, Dad gave Bhuaji the honour of naming all of us, and because she was Hindu, we were all given Hindu names. Many are confused by this, as we're actually Sikhs, but it not only showed how comfortable Dad was with Hinduism, but also how he held Bhuaji in such high regard.

Mum told me how Bharti was a highly honourable and patriotic Indian name and that my father loved my name the most out of all of us.

'Go ahead and change it if you want to,' she said, 'but you'll always be Bharti in my eyes and I won't call you Barbara, Parbara or Marbara, ever!' she added, using the names in a derogatory way.

That was the end of my quest to change my name.

Mum's insistence that my name remain Bharti did more than just quell a mere teenage rebellion. She enabled me to hold on to who I was by her refusal to let me take on another identity to escape the bullying. It meant I stayed true to who I was. What also helped was my parents' constant insistence that I was theirs, as it provided an anchor in stormy seas, giving me a sense of belonging, thereby shoring up my fragile sense of self. Their assertion that I was theirs led to them being unable to discuss my adoption when I was a child, but this was merely to protect me from feeling rejected if I got to know the truth. Mum explained that they didn't want me to feel I wasn't part of the family if I found out I was actually adopted. They chose to keep that from me and hoped I'd never find out the truth. And when we had to leave Uganda, my mother was even to risk her life to claim me as hers – her daughter.

In my extended family, our younger relatives call Anju '*masiji*', which means 'aunty'(mother's sister) and is a sign of respect given by a younger person to an older person. Yet, some of them call me just Bharti, which is so disrespectful. It may seem like a small aberration, but it feels significant to me, sending me a message that I'm not accepted within that part of the family. My sense of self-respect won't let me stoop to telling them how much this offends me. I wasn't always able to do this, however.

After many years of feeling angry and trying to work out ways to challenge them, often finding myself crying in bed after everyone else had gone to sleep and questioning why they addressed me that way, I had an epiphany: I realized *I* was the only one who was hurting. The incident with the Cinzano taught me that, too.

But as time has gone on and my sense of self and worth has grown, I can actually laugh to myself at the pettiness of it all now. I realize that I can decide *not* to be affected by their meanness. If they want to call me Bharti rather than my title, which is more respectful, then go for it...! This is because now, I can just witness their insensitivity on the outside and smile to myself on the inside. The only people who can hurt me are the ones who matter to me – those whose opinions count – not those who don't, or who don't play a large part in my life.

The biggest release for me was when I forgave them in my heart, as I realized that this was actually a reflection of their lack of worth and respect for themselves. Even now, when I meet them and they greet me using my name, I send a silent message of forgiveness towards them and offer blessings. After years of doing so, it's become much easier and, do you know, every time I do it with an open heart and genuine love, I feel my own worth and self-respect grow. One thing I appreciate in all this, however, is the truth. I'd rather they called me Bharti, because that tells me their true feelings, than for them to call me by my title and feign respect out of a sense of duty.

So you get the picture. All of my life, people seem to have disliked something or other about me. It might be because I'm black, female, the lupus, epidermolysis bullosa, whatever. But there is always the associated physical and emotional scars. Most importantly, I found ways to cope and decided that my worth would never be measured by other people – they make unreliable witnesses, after all. I came to realize that the views of others will be negative at times, but at other times they will be positive. Listening to their opinions left me feeling like I was on an emotional roller coaster of beautiful highs and ugly lows, inducing waves of both euphoria and depression in equal measure. It's taken me a long time to learn to be more open and more trusting. And in order to do so, I had to let go and turn to myself, to my inner strength and knowing, in order to find self-love and self-acceptance.

I've come to understand that when words hurt me, the other person is telling me something about themselves. People have said to me, 'You're just too sensitive,' or, 'You've got a chip on your shoulder.' To give you an example, I remember telling someone from an Indian background about an incident that involved me being called a 'black monkey'. I told them how I found some of the Indian community racist, believing beauty and worth are associated with lighter skin. This person replied that it sounded to them like I had a real chip on my shoulder. In their eyes, this was my problem and they didn't want to acknowledge it.

I see this now as a silencing tactic. The truth is, who is actually more sensitive – me, or that woman who couldn't bear to hear about my experience? It's really hard when people dismiss your reality, when they try to take away the worth of your experience because they're uncomfortable with your truth. If this situation ever arises now, I just hold on to my worth and remember that I don't have to fix the awkwardness of the situation, or make the other person feel better, especially when I feel that they've acted in a thoughtless or cruel way. Some people want to become the victim to avoid responsibility and deflect the hurt they've caused.

If something upsets me now, I ask myself if it's a small deal or a big deal. If I'm reacting strongly to minor issues, it may tell me that my worth is fragile. Sometimes that sense of fragility does creep in, where a small incident can become a bigger drama if I let it fester. Whenever I feel I'm losing perspective, I bring in compassion. I can now see that the person upsetting me is coming from a place of low self-worth. I can then reclaim my power by sending that person a blessing, asking my God to bless them with peace, joy or self-love – whatever I think they need. Then I ask God to bless my worth and take away the hurt.

I may not always get it right – I'm only human, after all, and I may well react with anger, which makes my worth shrivel and leaves me feeling nauseous and ashamed for the rest of the day. If that happens, I forgive myself. Self-forgiveness allows me to reclaim my worth.

I believe we all have a sense of worth inside us. And that sense of worth is the one that shouts out, 'Why me? Why am I being dealt this hand? Why is life so unfair? Why am I the one who has to experience this pain?' Worth isn't the negative voice that tells you you're worthless. Worth starts the very moment you start questioning – and it rises when you turn that question into a statement:

This isn't right.

I shouldn't be feeling this pain.

I shouldn't be treated like this.

I don't want to feel like this any more.

I don't want to be anxious.

I don't want to be depressed.

Worth rises between the question and the statement. A question may well feel helpless – Why me? – but it can also ignite resistance:

I don't accept this situation.

I won't put up with this treatment.

A better question would be to ask what you want instead, putting it into a positive light.

When you acknowledge your resistance, you create change. You change the way you're seeing yourself – not as a victim now, but as a warrior who knows their worth. So whether it's an illness, whether it's the way you're being treated or it's something that's happened, your sense of worth is the voice that says: 'No, that's not me. This is unfair.' Listen to that voice, because it will spur you into action to protect yourself, to stand firm and to grow strong. For before you can act against the negative situation or words, you need to rise up and say to the other person that they have no right to speak about or to you in this way. It's this realization that causes you to act and become stronger. Worth always feels alive – it's not a memory or a habitual thought form, like negative thoughts that swim around your head sometimes. It's not something that's static. It's a moveable achievement. Worth comes into your heart and tells you you're better than this. You're always good enough.

There were and still are moments when demons from my past raise their ugly heads and I find myself being transported back to the girl punching herself in the mirror. But now I put a smile on my face and whisper, 'Go away – you have no power over me.' And I will keep repeating this until it drowns out the negatives that creep in, which they sometimes will. Those words have nurtured the seeds of my worth and helped them to grow. And the more I repeat them, the easier it becomes to believe that those words are true. The more I believe, the more empowered I feel inside.

Today, I'll occasionally sense the shadow of old, hurtful words creeping in when meeting new people. For whatever reason, I'll decide that they're looking at me and thinking, *She's so ugly*. If that thought comes in, I know I'm projecting my old lack of self-worth onto them. So, I look that person in the eye and resolve not to dwell on any negative thoughts they may or may not be having about me. I just think, *I'm in the here and now and I'm God's child. I'm beautiful to*

God and I was made in God's image, so I'm not going to let negativity in. I still have to work at this and it's an ongoing process. Memories have a way of resurfacing, but a sense of worth can stop me from sliding back into old patterns of thinking and the pain those negative thoughts bring.

~

CHAPTER 13

A Spiritual Journey

Before I tell you this part of my story, please know that I understand how many people take comfort in religion and it's *not* my intention to criticize that choice. However, my focus here is to look at how the beliefs or traditions we adopt or are born into can either support or diminish our precious sense of worth. Of course, we cannot say that every individual represents the essence of the religion they follow. I can only speak from my own experience – first as a child, then later as an adult – of living with epidermolysis bullosa and lupus. And I'm grateful for those experiences, for without them I may never have found my own connection with the Divine.

My parents were Sikhs who also embraced Hinduism, so when I was a child, we regularly visited the Hindu temple in Kabale, as there was no gurdwara (Sikh temple). In Hinduism and Sikhism, it seemed to me that my illnesses were all about karma. I was ill because I'd done something wrong in my past life. The other view was that I thought I was above God and so the epidermolysis bullosa had come along to keep me grounded – two rather conflicting ideas. Both theories said I was to blame for my condition. I'd unknowingly done something wrong in a past life, or had the wrong idea about myself in this life.

My father urged us to attend Christian assemblies at school, believing it was important that we learn about Christianity. He'd constantly remind us of this fact when we mentioned that some classmates who were also of Asian heritage were exempted from attending at their parents' request. He was of the view that one day, we'd choose for ourselves what religion we wanted to follow. At least if we knew what each was all about, we could make an informed choice. For this reason, I was open to the teachings of Christianity. In terms of my illness, the teachers at my missionary school in Uganda taught us that faith in God and Jesus would heal me. All I needed was enough faith – so in that sense, I was responsible for curing myself through prayer. And when I wasn't healed, I blamed myself for not praying hard enough, not having enough faith, and even for betraying God by following another faith, as my family was Sikh. I reasoned that I shouldn't go to any other place of worship, as we'd been told God would be jealous if we went to other gods. Maybe that was one of the reasons I wasn't healed through prayers to the Christian God.

Both Hinduism and Sikhism sought to explain the reason for my disease, and it was through Hinduism that I realized the lessons I'd learned were down to a form of penance for wrong deeds in my past life, so that hopefully I might never have to endure such suffering in my next life. Sikhism taught me that I could be liberated by God's grace. Christianity would surely show me the way to a miracle cure.

When I went to Hull University, I committed to Christianity. I really wanted to be a good girl, to make my mum proud that I hadn't disgraced her in any way. I joined the Christian Union in order to meet other people with whom I felt would share equally moral values. I was concerned about getting in with the wrong crowd because the idea of honour was so indoctrinated in me – *when you go to university, do not bring shame on the family name.* Being part of a religious group gave me an identity: that of a nice moral girl. Little did I know how much it would impact my sense of worth.

In Uganda, I'd been used to Christian assemblies being rather dull affairs. The first time I attended a Pentecostal church was while I was at university and I was smitten. Friends explained that they believed that God and the Holy Spirit were present both during the service and in their personal lives. They said that faith was powerful and that, if I attended, I'd experience that power rather than focus on ritual or reflection. They explained that I'd feel God's presence during the worship.

And they were right. I loved the joy, the passion and the exuberance that the congregation demonstrated during the services. I loved the dancing and clapping and the upbeat music invariably played by a band at the front. The atmosphere was intoxicating. I experienced things I'd never seen in an Anglican or Methodist church. Frequenting a Pentecostal church was like attending a spiritual concert, leaving me yearning for yet more of that spiritual high.

And yet, I still questioned myself. I looked at other members going into a trancelike state during services – during which they'd begin by speaking in tongues (a sign that the Holy Spirit had taken over someone and the person had started speaking in a different language). They appeared to have some kind of transcendental experience and I'd wonder why the same wasn't happening to me. I truly believed in Jesus, God and the Holy Spirit in the way they did and had even been baptized, yet I wasn't called to speak in a different language. More importantly, I'd find myself wondering why I wasn't being healed. It was believed that even the common cold could be healed through prayer relatively quickly, perhaps even the next day, and sure enough, that formerly cold-ridden believer would invariably bounce up the next day saying, 'I prayed. I had faith. Now my cold is gone!'

Once, I asked one of my fellow Christian Union friends if God could make my nails grow once more. I was desperate to wear open-toed sandals and, being a typical young woman, my desire to coat them in nail polish was strong. She said that if I was to have faith and ask God, Jesus and the Holy Spirit to give me nails that my wish would be granted and they'd once again be beautiful. So I'd prayed fervently for nails and woke expectantly each day, completely sure that that would be the day I'd wake with nails once more.

I prayed for many months before those prayers petered out. Every time I questioned why my nails didn't come back, I was told I hadn't prayed hard enough, or that I didn't hold real faith, because even to have asked the question in the first place denoted a lack of belief or conviction. No one told me what I had to demonstrate to God to show that my faith was real. Some even said the nails wouldn't grow, as God didn't like so-called vanity.

That old message from my childhood came rushing back to me: *You're not cured because you don't have faith.* After a night of fervent praying, I'd wake the next morning thinking *It's today – finally, I'll be free of this disease.* Lying in bed, I'd feel my body for blisters and of course, they'd still be there. I wasn't cured. And I had the lupus to contend with, too. The impact of my constant failure to self-heal was so corrosive that I'd doubt myself. I'd find myself thinking, *How much more faith can I give God when nothing happens?* People were saying I didn't have enough faith and that that was why I was the way I was – and maybe they were right. But it was hard to hold faith when nothing happened and yet you truly believed.

I felt consumed by confusion and self-doubt. There was an implied punishment, too, as I struggled to relate to a God whose ego was so fragile that He'd strike me down or send me to hell if I didn't believe in Him enough. It seemed to me that all the tests God gave were geared to test people's faith in Him. As a result, I thought He was egotistical and cruel with some of the tests he gave. I knew this God well enough from school assemblies and the Bible story of Job. We'd often be reminded of how God had allowed Satan to destroy everything Job held dear – his ten children, his riches and his health. After Satan's interventions, he's depicted wearing a sackcloth and is afflicted with leprosy sores from head to toe (you can see why that part of the story resonated with me). He's reduced to nothing, yet still he doesn't blame God, and nor does he renounce Him. Eventually, God gives Job more than he'd lost – the moral of the story being that Job's faith is eventually rewarded and that suffering can be endured.

That story had a profound effect on me, as I immediately applied it to my own situation. *I don't want God to do that to me and destroy what I hold dear.* Family was so important to me, particularly as a child with no biological family that I knew of. I lived in fear that God would want to test my faith that way, slowly taking everything from me, so that eventually I'd be left with no family, no home and then nothing at all.

I already had epidermolysis bullosa, so in my eyes maybe God's punishment had already begun. I caught myself wondering why God would want to do that. I didn't understand how He could be so cruel. How much could one person endure in a lifetime? I'd already been abandoned as a baby. Did God do that, too, to test me? Ultimately, I was brought up to believe that this God had supreme power. And yet, if He had the power to destroy, surely He could heal.... I still wanted to believe that.

Healing services were a regular feature of the Pentecostal churches and those dedicated services always drew a big crowd. We'd begin with prayers, asking the Holy Spirit to come down into the congregation, which would be followed by the pastor inviting people to come forwards for healing by the laying-on of hands. A great shuffling would break out as people emerged from the pews either on foot, on crutches or in wheelchairs, all heading towards the pulpit for the so-called miracle cure. Some even came with names and photographs of loved ones asking for healing on their behalf.

The pastor would place his hands on top of their heads, saying in turn, 'In the name of the Father, the Son and the Holy Spirit, you are healed. You are free from pain.' Then he'd name the ailment they suffered from, such as MS or cancer, or any other condition they might have, saying that they were free from it, followed by a final 'Praise God. Hallelujah.'

Each person in turn wept and shouted in gratitude for having been healed. They'd be cheering and echoing the pastor's words as the church band played on.

'Praise God! Hallelujah!'

During one such ceremony, a warm feeling coursed through my body the moment the pastor laid his hands over the crown of my head. Like others before me, I wanted to be free from pain. I just knew there was something in that warmth, believing it to be the healing I so craved. I needed to *believe* I'd been healed so that healing would follow. Not believing depicted lack of faith, so I forced myself to say it, making it more real. People shouted hallelujah in true Gospel form, one of jubilance, with the congregation all beaming at me when it was my turn, cheering, stamping and clapping. The pastor raised his hands and instructed me to throw my medicine away!

So I didn't take my medicine for two days and, as a result, my joints were weighted with pain. By the third day I was in such agony that I couldn't even move, let alone get out of bed. As soon as I went back on my steroids and immunosuppressants, the inflammation in my joints ebbed and I began to feel better. Of course, the healing hadn't worked, but I was convinced it had. But then because I'd kept my medicine to hand rather than thrown it away, surely that spelled a lack of faith.

Here's how it went after that: each time I went back to church, I could guarantee that someone would state that I'd been healed. So I could either hide my blisters and nod, agreeing with them that I'd been healed of both conditions, for I didn't want people to think otherwise. Or, the other scenario: I could say I wasn't yet cured and that I still had blisters. But I knew what their reaction would be – that the blisters were a test and that I still had to believe that I'd been healed.

If I was again to say that I wasn't healed, they'd say things like: 'Oh, that's the devil. That's Satan telling you that you haven't been healed.' In their eyes, I was letting Satan take control.

If I admitted was still on medication, they'd say, 'That's a sign you don't have enough faith. If you can't throw your medicine away, you'll never be healed.'

But whatever I did or didn't do, I was indeed guilty of faithlessness.

Still, I tried. I found other healing services to go to, places where people didn't know me. But you guessed it – neither prayers nor healing did anything to improve my condition. Whatever I did or didn't do, it seemed I wasn't good enough to be healed. I couldn't understand why God wasn't blessing me in this way by restoring good health. Some people may well have been healed through faith, but what about the rest of us – those who hadn't been?

It left me questioning myself and my beliefs, maintaining my conviction that I was so worthless in God's eyes that I wasn't to be blessed with healing. But this way of thinking was dispiriting and disempowering. Although I understand that healing through faith may give people a sense of self-empowerment, it has quite the opposite effect if those prayers don't work. I can also see how my need to find a cure, wanting God or the Holy Spirit or whoever to fix me, was symptomatic of my low self-esteem at that time.

I remember going to one Pentecostal church for a healing service. This time, I chose not to go up for healing and decided just to remain an observer. This was towards the end of my relationship with the Christian Church, when I was beginning to see I'd never be one of the chosen ones. During the ritual, one of the pastors had a child who was very disabled. Holding up the child before the congregation, the pastor called out, 'In the name of Jesus, this child will be healed. The Holy Spirit has come down on this child.'

The pastor and his wife held the child in an attempt to get him to walk, but when he still couldn't, instead they pulled him along so his legs had to follow, excitedly proclaiming 'See! He's been healed, he's been healed!' I remember thinking, *But he's not been healed – he's still got this disability.* I immediately felt a rush of guilt: how could I possibly be thinking something like this in a place of worship! No wonder there was no healing for me here, for I didn't believe – I was one of the doubters.

The final fracture in my faith came at another Pentecostal church I'd started attending in my early twenties when I was living in Wolverhampton, after leaving Hull University. There, I told a pastor's wife something very personal about my past and she asked if I wanted her to tell her husband. I explained that I was telling her as a woman and that I wanted it to stay between us.

The following week, this same pastor gave a sermon about how the devil can come into a couple's relationship. As I was listening to him, I realized he was referring to me. He preached that husbands and wives should never keep secrets from one another, and how his wife had been told to keep a particular secret from him. He interpreted this as an evil influence – this was surely the devil at work! He believed that the devil had expertly used a person (me) to drive a wedge between husband and wife. I felt so humiliated

– he didn't name me, but I knew he was calling me out because I didn't want his wife to discuss my past. I couldn't believe how he could turn my need for support into a shameful secret. Imagine the horror I felt....

Determined not to let the pastor see how his sermon had affected me, I forced myself to continue going back to that church. It was November, around the time of Bonfire Night. Another pastor stood up, saying how he was annoyed because the council had refused permission for them to hold a bonfire on the land next to the church. He was so angry that he even wanted to burn down the building next door – which happened to be an Indian restaurant – and use that for firewood. Everybody stood up and clapped in agreement. I sat there, looking straight ahead. *I don't belong here*, I thought, so I walked out and never went back to that church.

I then went on to Leicester to study social work. While I was at university doing my MA degree, Mum was racially harassed and threatened. We'd moved from the peace of our first house to another area in Berkshire. This came about because we needed more room after Shankerdas got married and had children. There were nine of us under one roof, so Mum, Anju, Mina, Shiv and I moved out. At the time, it seemed like a positive move, and when I came home during the holidays, I was delighted with our new place – it was a corner house, big enough for all of us, with a tree in the front garden. That's when all the trouble began. Mum had only been settled a month when the attacks started.

One evening, we were sitting in the living room at the back of the house – the kitchen was in the front, overlooking the road – when all of a sudden there was a mighty crash. A brick had been put through the kitchen window! We had no idea why it had happened, or who was responsible. The same thing happened the next night, only this time a brick was put through Mina's bedroom window. If she'd been in bed at the time, the brick would have landed on her pillow – or worse, her head. It was terrifying. Mum moved Mina's bed closer to the window the next night, as we figured that if it happened again, the brick would invariably travel towards the other side of the room, thereby missing her. That didn't solve the problem of the glass from the window shattering on top of Mina as she slept, though.

Every time I phoned home from university, it seemed there had been another incident. The harassment was non-stop. Even when Mum took a shortcut through the park to the bus stop to catch a bus to town, children would run after her and kick her as she walked. These children were really young – perhaps four- and five-year olds. All she wanted to do was go into town to do some shopping. She even had my brother with her, but still it didn't stop them as she held his hand.

The local youths taunted Mum, too, shouting obscenities like 'Pakis out', and 'Piss off back where you came from.' There was name-calling, all of it. Graffiti was plastered over our front door depicting similar profanities, and dog excrement posted through the letter box. Even an elderly man, who looked pleasant enough, deliberately let his dog defecate in our front garden. Each and every day, he opened our garden gate, shooed the dog into the garden and waited for it to leave its unwanted gift as we watched on, helpless, from the kitchen window. He'd stare back at us with a sly, taunting expression, as if daring us to say or do something. But our instincts told us that if we did anything, we'd probably be threatened or attacked by people he knew, so we remained quiet and did nothing.

It all culminated in a fire. Someone ripped off a branch from the tree in our garden, placed it against the front door and set it alight. Mum had heard a noise and seen what they were doing, so she'd run from the house with a jug of water to douse the flames before the branch was fully ablaze. If she hadn't done so, she and my siblings could have been trapped in the house or even died.

Every time I got a call at university, I was terrified it would be the police informing me that my family had been killed. I dreaded the phone ringing. Something had to be done before someone was seriously injured or worse. Anju was married by now. She and her husband, Murli, sold their house in Hampshire, but instead of going to their new home in Berkshire, they decided to move back in with Mum, Shiv and Mina, hoping a male presence in the home would deter the attacks. While they did lessen, it was by no means a complete stop. Every time a window was smashed, Murli would run out of the house only to see the perpetrators speeding away in a car. It was always late at night, always in a car, not on foot, and so hard to catch the number plates.

The police would come, but because there was no evidence that it had been a racist attack, they couldn't do anything. The only time the police acknowledged our plight was when explicit graffiti was plastered on the property saying 'Pakis out' and 'Yur not welcum here.' The illiteracy and spelling was on another level.

I wrote to the council for months pleading with them to move our family elsewhere, but nothing happened. Then the morning after the night of the attempted arson, my mother had gone to hospital for an appointment. She hadn't had a wink of sleep all night and her consultant, seeing her plight, wrote to the council insisting we were moved owing to the adverse effect the stress was having on her health. If anything was to happen to Mum, he said he'd hold them personally responsible. The council moved us a few weeks later, and Murli and Anju returned to their new home in Berkshire, which had lain vacant while they were living with Mum. We were sent to a nicer, more diverse area of the town, and I've lived here ever since.

I couldn't understand why Mum never retaliated – why she didn't shout or run after them. She'd cry afterwards, but she never lashed out or responded in any way. She ran that gauntlet of hate every day and never complained just got on with it, accepting her lot. The police couldn't do anything as she couldn't give a description of her attackers because they'd always come under the darkness of night. They'd come by car and hurl bricks or get out their aerosols and daub graffiti everywhere then speed off, so no one was ever apprehended for the abuse we suffered. But still, Mum would say, 'You don't know what weakness made them do this. You don't know what was going on in their lives to make them do this.' She was so resilient and forgiving....

We were in that house for two years – two years of daily harassment and victimization. But Mum somehow generated a sense of compassion for the abusers – all those kids and youths, even the old man and his dog. She saw them as weak people merely looking to feel more powerful at others' expense.

There was another Asian family on our road, just two doors down from us. Amazingly, they were also from our hometown of Kabale,

Uganda. They'd listen when Mum told them what was going on, but they couldn't help. The racists left them alone and if they got involved, they, too, would no doubt have become a target. Perhaps they didn't touch them because they had a disabled child and the rule of bullies meant a disabled child was off limits. Either that, or perhaps it was because the child's father was a bus driver and so may have been seen more as part of the community. Maybe our harassers hated us because of that. But Mum never blamed that family for not wanting to get involved – for they clearly had their own reasons.

Similarly, even an English family who were initially friendly towards us backed off when they realized the extent of the abuse we were under. If Mum knocked on their door for help, they often didn't answer, even though we knew they were home because we could see them through the living room window. Ultimately, Mum had no neighbours or anyone to whom to turn at times like these, and she felt incredibly alone and isolated. But still, she always said: 'Don't judge them, because you don't know what they've been through.' She didn't believe that anyone was born evil – not even the soldiers we encountered on our way out of Uganda. Mum could always see a false show of strength for the weakness it truly was.

So, the harassment and racially motivated attacks at home in Berkshire, along with the racist comments in the Pentecostal church, brought me to a crisis point with Church pastors in general. I vowed never to enter any other church again. Maybe I shouldn't have had such high expectations of human beings, but I couldn't accept that level of cruelty and lack of acceptance or compassion in what was supposedly the home of God – a church. Especially not from people who professed to be brothers and sisters in Christ and therefore all equal in God's eyes. These weren't the people physically abusing us on the council estate – they were supposed to be better than that… yet it was abuse all the same, whatever way you looked at it.

In the Sikh gurdwaras and Hindu temples, I'd had people point at me because of my African heritage. I'd walk in and hear the whispers of my mother or father's alleged infidelities. Then there would be the sniggers. And if I got talking to people and told them I was adopted, they didn't believe me, so I soon realized the futility of saying anything.

I felt so sorry for Mum, hearing those horrible comments. They evidently thought that the only explanation for my existence had to be an affair. In their eyes, no one would actually *choose* to adopt a black girl, so the story of my adoption had to be a way of concealing my dad's alleged infidelity. Even then, if I were really adopted, why would my parents choose such a dark child?

In our Indian community, I knew people found it hard to accept their own birth children if they were dark-skinned. The worst thing that could happen to any woman was giving birth to a girl – for what they wanted was sons – never mind one who had dark skin. At least if she was fair, she was considered marriageable, but it would be harder to find a husband who would accept a dark-skinned girl.

I remember Mum telling me off once when she heard me say I was adopted to a couple of women in the gurdwara. As far as she was concerned, I was her daughter and that's all they needed to know. If they wanted to use their dirty minds to think their dirty thoughts, she saw that as their problem. She wasn't going to sit there and justify her actions to anybody, especially as it wasn't anyone else's concern.

When I look back, I realize how strong she was. She knew that saying I was adopted brought disbelief, instant disapproval or faint praise disguised as kindness: how wonderful my parents were to have taken on a child like me. So she refused to tell people I was adopted just to satisfy them and I saw real power in that – and that was a lesson for me. I shouldn't have to explain myself to others just to satisfy their agendas.

In the gurdwaras, we'd sit together for *langhar* – a communal meal at which men and women eat together to show equality – but I'd hear people asking questions about me being black and why I was there. In social situations, I've also heard families asking each other about caste – although being a Sikh should mean you reject the idea of caste entirely. For me, it's also ironic that people revere Lord Krishna's foster parents – Yashoda and Nandagopa (who brought up Lord Krishna as if he were their biological son) – but refuse to recognize the worth of children adopted by families 'not of their blood'. It seems like the doctrines don't match the actions, in that there was a sense of intense judgement, which I found discomforting and unacceptable.

The result was that I couldn't bear to enter a Hindu temple or a gurdwara, and by my early twenties, I'd turned my back on the Christian Church. My options were limited as I wondered where I'd turn next, for I had God, but I didn't have a church. I loved devotional singing – the *shabads* at the Sikh gurdwaras (hymns within the Sikh scriptures), the Hindu *bhajans* (congregational singing and bonding) and the Christian hymns – and felt sadness at leaving that music behind. But I knew I had to believe in something, because my life was a miracle from day one.

I sensed and believed a Divine presence had protected me and been with me throughout my life – there was no other explanation for my survival – but I had no idea what my spiritual path should be outside mainstream religion. I felt that I didn't belong anywhere. I'd been uprooted from Uganda at twelve, just after my father died, and then we'd come to England with the many other families who were similarly traumatized by Idi Amin's policy of Asian expulsion. As a student away from home for the first time, I'd turned to the Church as a place of refuge, so, one way or another, I felt it had rejected me, too, through that sermon where a pastor decided God had told Him I had come to cause a rift between him and his wife, and then that racist reference to wanting the Indian restaurant to burn down.

I had to make sense of why it had come to this – why the doors of those churches and temples had become closed to me emotionally. It was during this period that I remembered a small incident: how a light had appeared in my room at university in the depths of the night. I was terrified of the dark and wasn't used to sleeping on my own. I'd even slept with the light on for the first two nights until I made myself turn it off.

This particular night, I'd said a prayer like every night before trying to sleep, feeling really scared about being in the dark. The next thing I knew, I felt a wave of comfort wash over me under that ethereal light. It lasted just a few seconds, but afterwards I could sleep with the light off without any fear. It was as if the light said to me, 'I'm always here – there's nothing for you to worry about.'

It took me many years to understand that loving presence, to understand that God was still with me, and to see my survival as a series of angelic interventions that had guaranteed my strange and at times fragile existence.

Today, I'm not looking for religion. Instead, I'm beginning to feel my way towards a spirituality that rests upon a personal relationship with God and my guardian angel. When I stopped looking for answers outside myself, I felt what I can only describe as a gentle awakening to spirit. That may sound simplistic, but the sheer relief of giving up that search allowed something more loving and beautiful to come in. I began to feel a new connection with God – and a deeper connection to my soul. I was worth something, after all, and I didn't need mainstream religion to validate or test me any longer.

In fact, the traditions of holding faith that I'd followed had at times undermined whatever worth I'd tried to build. My worth had been eroded through the teachings that my illness was caused by misdemeanours committed in my past life, or by saying I didn't have enough faith to be healed. Whatever the message, it wore away my sense of worth, as I believed that nothing I could do was enough to be worthy of being cured by God.

I kept listening to the guidance I felt and realized that I wasn't being guided towards another religion – that instead, guidance itself was my faith and my belief. I could have my own unconditional relationship with the angels and with whom I perceived God to be. I'd had something I could trust and believe in right inside me all along that wasn't attached to just one faith or one building. My soul told me that my worth wasn't tied up in those buildings or in those people, either. I knew it was angels that would always guide and protect me. It was that angelic protection that had saved me many times before I became a young woman, and I came to realize that it was to continue into adulthood.

My guardian angels were clearly at work when driving home for the first time from Leicester University. The road was dark and rain was coming down in sheets. I was in a line of cars travelling along a narrow country road near Oxford, when I saw a car starting to overtake on the opposite side of the road. To my horror, I realized it was going to hit the two cars in front of me. I was so busy being anxious and afraid for the occupants of the cars in front that I didn't realize they'd swerved violently into a hedge to avoid being hit. Now, the car was coming straight at me!

I froze.

Then I felt my steering wheel being wrenched to the left at the last second before impact. The oncoming car wrecked my bonnet, but I was okay. In the melee that followed – with drivers running over, questions being asked and recriminations mixed with apologies being uttered from the driver who'd caused the crash – I remained in a confused daze.

The police later told me that it was a miracle I turned when I did, praising me for my quick thinking and judgment. If I hadn't turned at that precise time, I'd have been hit head on, and with the speed the other driver was going, I could easily have been killed, apparently. If I'd turned too quickly, he'd have undoubtedly crushed or killed me, as the impact would have been on the driver's door. It was then that I praised and thanked my guardian angel, because in my heart I knew that all I'd done was freeze in shock – it was them who'd saved me, not me. Perhaps they'd even saved the other driver, as it was a miracle none of us were hurt that day.

Another example of being protected was when I took to walking in the early hours of the morning. I needed to meditate and tune in to guidance, and the only way to make the time to do that, given my existing schedule, would be at the beginning of the day. I'd leave the house at 6 a.m. and begin my walking meditation by meandering past a quiet industrial yard and a patch of woodland that led to a grid of suburban houses. This particular circular route was well-lit – it was often dark when I'd begin the walk – and I loved to immerse myself in the peace and silence, watching the sky lighten as dawn approached and the sun rose over the rooftops. I'd tune in to any spiritual messages that might come in and give thanks for all I had. This was a time to be with myself, with my God and my angels, before the responsibilities of the day took hold. And I always felt safe.

After seven months of these early-morning walks, I began to get an eerie feeling and a message coming through: *Don't do this walk, it's dangerous.* I decided maybe it was just me and that I was making excuses, but then the sense of danger intensified and the messages became more insistent. I felt my guardian angel telling me, *'Don't do this. Don't go there.'* Yet still I ignored it, because I'd set myself the task of walking 3 km (two miles) every day and there was no reason to feel unsafe that I knew of. I'd always felt protected, and walking the more isolated parts of my route – past the small wooded area with a path shrouded by trees and bushes – had never bothered me before.

Then a severe chest infection left me unable to go outside for three weeks. And it was then that I heard a woman had been raped in the early hours of the morning. And guess what – she'd been attacked in that exact woodland location that I walked past every morning.... My heart went out to her and her family, and I finally understood why I'd received that premonition. And because I hadn't listened, my body had done it for me.

Since that time, I've called upon angels to help me many times during prayers to God. While strong messages still come in to protect me, I've begun to see that I can reach out for help for other reasons, and that the angels will listen.

Just a few months ago, I was feeling really desperate. As a single parent, money can be tight, but this time my mood was very low about my financial situation. I sent up a prayer, trusting that I'd receive guidance.

'Angels, if you're with me in this, just give me a sign that you're around, supporting me, because at the moment I feel so desperate and alone.'

Shortly afterwards, I got in the car with my daughter to drive her to school, when she came across a pure-white feather on the dashboard. There was no way it could have got in the car, as my windows were up as it was winter. And then I thought, *That's a sign the angels are with me, letting me know I'm not alone.* I began to realize that all I'd been focusing on was my dire financial situation rather than the blessings of having a salary coming in, having family and friends, a home and material comforts. I changed my thinking to attract positivity – *I've got a job, I've got work, I've got money coming in, I am blessed.*

A solution came soon after. A young girl from India looking for a room to rent came to me via my brother and sister-in-law, who asked if I'd take her in. It wasn't a huge amount of money, but it was enough to take the weight of worry from my mind. That solution helped to carry me through and is still an option I can look to should the need ever arise once more. I believe the angels and God heard my prayer that day and that feather was sent to say, 'We're here. We're listening to you. All will be well.'

I talk to my angels every time I wake and before I go to sleep. I ask for them to keep us safe on a long drive, and I pray to God and the angels to resolve any conflict with family or friends. And I'm open to the messages I receive. Every day I work with those messages, even if I don't want to hear them. They may ask me to confront a situation I'd rather avoid, or for me not to wallow in self-pity. I know some people may think these examples are small and that it's nothing significant, but it means something to me. Living with lupus, epidermolysis bullosa and all the issues around my race, gender and identity, I've learned to appreciate every tiny thing I have.

My lupus is largely under control these days, owing to the medication I take, and my epidermolysis bullosa has improved, too. Since my mum buried that egg that day, I truly believe a level of healing took place, for the blisters never came back with the same intensity. When my lupus flares up or the very occasional blister comes up, I no longer pray for healing as I did during my Christian years. I'll talk to God and the angels because this affirms my worth, but I don't plead for a miracle cure. I've let go of so much fear – and I realize my illness was exacerbated by stress.

I do everything I can in terms of self-care. I ensure I get enough sleep, I make time for meditation and I listen to any guidance I receive in whatever form. If it feels right, I also engage in Reiki sessions (Reiki is a form of palm healing that unblocks the energy within the body). Once my blocks are removed, the flow of energy heals the pain I have in my joints, as well as removing my extreme tiredness from lupus. I can literally sleep through the whole session and wake feeling refreshed and soothed. I get such a feeling of empowerment from Reiki because it's offered me a way to understand myself more deeply, giving me the opportunity to connect to my worth emotionally, physically and spiritually.

Since childhood, I've experienced my inner sense of worth as a strong sensation in the pit of my stomach. Just before I have that feeling, I might receive messages saying things along the lines of 'This situation is wrong' or, 'You're worth much more than this.' The angel message encourages me to let my worth rise. It gives me permission to challenge anything that doesn't feel right.

I'm not a person who likes to challenge – instead, I prefer to be silent or to walk away. But when a message comes in saying I need to take action, I've learned to trust it and allow my worth to build. It's a physical thing, where I can feel it rising to my heart and then my throat, at which point I know I'm speaking from a place of self-belief, because when you take the time to tune in to the angelic guidance around you, you find the strength to get those words out.

It helps me to turn a negative situation into a positive on the spot. So often, we don't feel able to do anything when faced with a challenge – we're too busy processing what's happening in the immediate moment. But then the moment passes and we're left feeling vulnerable, passive, as if we've let something significant go unchallenged.

When I was a child, I went into a shop one day to hear an exchange between two assistants. One commented, 'She has lovely earrings, hasn't she?' referring to the gold hoop earrings my mother had given me. The other replied, 'She must have stolen them – that's how people like her get to wear gold like that.' They were speaking in Punjabi and assumed I wouldn't understand as I looked African. I left the shop without a word.

But as I got older, I saw that I needed to exercise my worth – not in a defensive way, but to claim my value so that I might be spoken about fairly, to be seen as equal and without prejudice. To give you an example, when I meet new people within our Asian community, they often assume I'm African–Caribbean. After chatting to the rest of my family in Punjabi, they'll then turn to me and talk in painful broken English. I'll reply in Punjabi and they'll look astonished that a woman who looks like me can speak their language. Speaking Punjabi confirms my place in my family – I grew up speaking both English and Punjabi. Replying in English while everyone else converses in Punjabi would have separated me from my family group, so this small act makes a big statement for me.

There have been moments of humour, too. At an Indian restaurant once, we sat down and ordered our food. One particular friend of mine ordered a certain curry and the waiter turned to his colleague and said in Punjabi, 'We don't have that dish.'

'Give her this other dish,' came the shameless reply. 'She'll never know.'

'That's not what was ordered,' I said in English when the dish arrived at the table.

'You're mistaken, ma'am – this is definitely what was ordered,' the waiter said firmly.

'I know exactly what this dish should be and I understood precisely what was said earlier,' I replied in Punjabi.

He looked embarrassed and took the dish away, apologizing profusely.

The way I react now to situations is a world away to how I felt as a child in that shop when the women had discussed my earrings so brazenly. Now, I've found I've become more able to challenge things when it's important. I don't believe this is about ego – it's about authenticity.

Worth isn't tied up in ego. It's not worth when you challenge someone from a position of anger, irritation or malice – that's ego. Worth comes from a place of compassion. If I were to oppose someone because of hate or a desire for revenge, it would have meant ego had taken over. Ego wants more ego, so it's unsurprising that some individuals build theirs by putting other people down.

When my inner voice says that I have to protect myself by challenging a situation, I do my best to connect with that person with compassion. Their behaviour may be down to a personal experience they had, or because they simply lack empathy – and I tell myself that it has little to do with me. I tell myself that that person is actually in a really bad place. And if I ever find it hard to generate compassion, I listen to the guidance from my angels, for it's they who give us the strength to show our worth in a compassionate way.

When you can keep compassion alive for someone who has hurt you, you can forgive them. Forgiveness isn't condoning their actions

– nor is it agreeing to be a physical or verbal punchbag. It's possible to forgive when you see that person as another human being who is suffering. I find myself thinking, *You're in such a bad place that you can't see the effect of your words and actions, so I can only forgive you because you don't know what you're doing.* Recognizing that they haven't evolved yet is a form of self-care. Being able to see from the forgiveness perspective creates distance between you – you become the observer rather than the victim.

If you find that hard, remember that this person isn't showing you their whole selves. When that individual is hating or rejecting something, they're only projecting what they themselves have been subjected to, as that's the way they've learned to react to certain situations from their own negative experiences. I pray that they're released from the turmoil, anger or bitterness that chains their souls, so their self-love and self-worth can grow – for their souls are chained by any inner turmoil, resentment, rage or hate. After all, how can one grow spiritually when these things hold them back and, by default, stop their souls from evolving?

My mum really believed this and she lived by it. She could never hate and always forgave – another lesson learned.

Recently, I read an article about people who had chosen to cut their parents out of their lives. One case study included the phrase, 'For my sense of worth, I had to cut myself off from them completely.' The individual went on to express their anger and bitterness against their family and stated how they'd hate them forever. I felt very sorry for that person, because to me it seemed they were mistaken – not in their decision to sever ties with their parents, but because they believed that their worth would be protected by doing so without forgiveness. When you're stuck in a place of anger, hatred and rejection, I believe your self-esteem cannot grow. When you can separate yourself while forgiving those who have hurt you, your worth can only grow. You've moved beyond the hurt inner child who is stuck and in pain to a place of self-confidence and self-respect.

If I could talk to that person, I'd say to them, 'Yes, your parents may have done you wrong, and nobody's going to condone them if they've abused you in any way, but the important thing is that your worth grows through forgiveness and compassion, and for you to develop as a human being.' When the child wants to reclaim their self-esteem by hurting their parents in return, their sense of worth doesn't grow because it remains stuck in a place of hate and anger. And in the end, no one feels worthy.

I've come to realize that worth is an active choice for me. I don't need to count my past successes or failures and give myself a rating. Worth doesn't rest on how much I earn, how healthy I am, or how much faith I have. Worth is for all of us, unconditional.

The more your worth grows, the more empowered you feel. Of course, we all need help from time to time – but other people are *not* responsible for giving you your self-esteem. We need to do that for ourselves by believing that we *are* worthy.

It's taken me many, many years to accept myself and my life story, and to acknowledge my worth. I've come to a point at which I recognize God as a Him or Her – and that God is what you want Him or Her to be. I'm more comfortable with a God who is loving and spiritual – not the punitive Old Testament version of God I was brought up to believe in at missionary school. Nor is it found in the religious doctrines that said, 'Yes, God can be loving and kind, but He can punish you, too.' This God rejects you if you don't believe in Him – or don't believe in Him enough. If you don't believe in His son, if you're gay, if you're a woman who has committed adultery (and therefore should be stoned to death), or any other behaviour that breaks a written or unwritten rule.

I found my version of God – a god who is both mother and father, and a being who can come in any form or guise. I can have a personal relationship with my God, both of us talking and listening to each other. The doctrines aren't for me now. I don't have to go to a church, a temple, a gurdwara or any religious building to prove my love and spiritual connection to my God, for I now know I have my own heart-and-soul connection. All I ever wanted was to feel I was worth something in my God's eyes. Now, I have a personal relationship with my God – and I feel free and at peace at last.

~

CHAPTER 14

Finding My Calling

My dream was always to become a journalist. I loved reading books and I enjoyed writing, but at 17 I changed my mind and decided to become a lawyer (one of the professions of choice for children of Indian parents). After my dad's death, while Mum was happy for all of us to be educated, there was no pressure on her side for me to study law. I got an A in A-level law, which I was really pleased about, giving me the confidence to apply for a law degree at Hull University.

The law course turned out to be full, so instead Hull offered me a place on a social sciences course, which covered some aspects of law – a criminology module, childcare law and criminal law – so I accepted, thinking it would be a good foundation for a law degree afterwards. After graduating, I again thought about taking a law degree, but I was worried about money. I had no intention of moving anywhere but home after finishing my BA degree, but once again, Destiny had other plans.

Friends told me about a vacancy in a centre that led to a job offer as a community advice worker in Wolverhampton. The pay was £3,000 a year and I was ecstatic, having had no sense of direction regarding what I might do after finishing my degree. Not only did I end up in the Midlands, something I'd never even considered, but it also felt like my job had literally fallen into my lap. I felt blessed and I felt rich! For the first time, I'd be earning my own money. When I'd had holiday jobs in the past, I always gave my small wage to Mum for my keep and she'd give me a small allowance in return, but this would be my first real pay packet.

I fitted into the Wolverhampton team really well, giving advice on benefits and getting to know the clients. I also set up a support group for Asian women coming into the centre who were suffering from domestic abuse, meaning they could talk about their experiences and draw comfort from each other. (My commitment to supporting survivors was to continue for many years, for I later volunteered in a refuge in Berkshire, spending eleven years on the committee for Sahara Women's Refuge. Protecting women's rights to live in a society that recognizes their worth is a cause that has always been close to my heart.)

Then my manager at the centre recommended I apply for a social-work secondment and an MA in social work, which the local authority would pay for. I'd said prayers asking for help and now my prayers had been answered – here was an opening. I then prayed I'd be accepted. At this stage I'd left the Church, but this was sure-fire proof of my worth to the Divine, because my prayers were still being answered. I was still being blessed and my needs were still being met even though I wasn't following a particular religion.

Together with my application form, I sent a stamped addressed envelope in the hope of receiving a reply as to whether or not I'd been successful. I knew there would be lots of applicants and I couldn't bear to have to ring up – or worse, not hear anything. It turned out that there were 500 applications for just three posts. To my delight, I was shortlisted and secured one of the jobs. Even better, I could start my Masters in two months' time.

I was over the moon. One of the reasons they said they'd chosen me was because I'd included this stamped addressed envelope. Apparently, I was the only one who sent one, showing that I'd thought about someone else and how I could make their life easier. I still laugh at this now and always include one with any subsequent job application.

As soon as I began in my new role, I realized I liked social work. It became my career and through it I was to meet Maryam – a work colleague who would later play a crucial role in leading me to adopt a child of my own.

I've always worked with vulnerable people. Even my holiday jobs were in care environments such as hospitals, perhaps because of my own familiarity with health services. One of my jobs was cleaning in a secure residential unit – a hospital for adults who were thought to have mental health problems, when in reality mainly they'd been born with severe developmental delay. You'd see grown men in cots and teenagers with a very low developmental age. Some could walk, others couldn't, and they were completely dependent on the staff. They were incarcerated in the unit because, at that time, during the 1970s, no other options were provided. These days, they'd receive more support and wouldn't be placed in a secure hospital, with no chance of ever leaving, without good reason.

I felt a lot of compassion for one young girl I'll call Anna for the purposes of this book, to protect her identity. Anna had learning disabilities and was on the autism spectrum. What was touching was that her family did love her, demonstrated by the fact they used to visit her every weekend. Sometimes they'd even collect her and take her home with them, bringing her back to the unit on a Sunday at teatime. Some patients had been rejected from a very early age and had no family coming to visit them at all, so in that respect Anna was lucky.

Although Anna may not have had any speech ability, her face used to light up when the weekend came round and her family arrived to take her home for those two days. Somehow, she just knew it was the weekend. You could see her excitement – she'd be pacing up and down by the window with a huge smile on her face because she knew her brother and parents were coming. I also remember Anna so vividly because she was about my age at the time – 19 – although her mental age was much younger.

These young men and women didn't have much quality of life and I used to feel so sad that they could never really feel free. They were entirely dependent on others for their care, and even if they could walk for themselves, they still had to be escorted everywhere, even in the hospital grounds. It was like a prison.

I knew what it was to feel helpless and my heart went out to those people. When I'd been in hospital with lupus for six months, I began to distinguish between the nurses who came to feed me. Some didn't ask me what I wanted to eat. It was a chore to them, so they'd shove everything on one fork – meat, veg, potato – and try to put it in my mouth. They didn't look at me and made it plain they were anxious to get going. I felt like they didn't want to be there feeding me. I felt like I was stopping them from having their own lunch or going on to their next task. I sensed that they were just doing it under sufferance and that I was imposing on them. Then there were those who fed me and asked what I'd like on my fork next. They gave me a choice – and that made me feel respected. They took the time to find out how I'd choose to eat if I were feeding myself. I saw the same thing at the secure unit, where I witnessed some nurses taking their time feeding the patients and others not.

Anna loved to have her hair brushed and would put ribbons and clips in it to feel pretty. Some nurses would come in and do her hair quickly, whereas others would ask her if she'd like plaits that day and what colour ribbon she wanted. You could see the smile on her face when a nurse took the trouble to give her a choice, to ask her opinion. Even though she couldn't speak, she was still able to choose the colour of ribbon she wanted in her hair, and her excitement was touching. That really resonated with me. Being the cleaner, no one saw what I noticed, but I really cared about patients being given the respect they deserved.

There was also a young man in a nappy, who I'll call Ali for the purposes of this book. Whenever I noticed he needed his nappy changing, I'd fetch one of the nurses. Some nurses attended to him straight away, while others said, 'In a minute,' which could mean anything from right now to an hour or so later. I'd gone through exactly the same thing in hospital, too, when I'd been admitted, where I'd had to ask to use the bedpan when I couldn't get out of bed because of my muscle atrophy and locked joints. All I wanted to do was get up and use the bathroom myself, but I couldn't, entirely reliant on others.

What I can say with certainty is that it makes you feel so powerless when a nurse doesn't give you any dignity, by making you wait. I couldn't even reach the bell on my bedside table, so I'd have to call out so everyone would know my business, or one of the other patients would ring the bell for me and tell the nurse I needed to go to the toilet. That 'minute' could mean ten minutes, half an hour or an hour, by which time it was too late and they'd have to change both me and the bed by then. It made me feel so humiliated. The nurses who'd bring the bedpan immediately also brought with them a certain respect, love and tenderness. I could feel it.

After my experience as a patient, I vowed that I'd treat everyone I met with compassion and dignity from that moment on. Everybody is worthy of respect, love and kindness, and it's important to remember that we could well be in that position ourselves one day. At 16, before I was diagnosed with lupus, I never imagined I wouldn't be able to move out of bed and that I'd have to rely on others to bathe and feed me. I've always carried that thought through into my life as a social worker. Every baby, child and adult should feel they're worth protecting, that they're worthy of respect, and that someone will listen to their story.

When I started out in social work, I worked with adults in the community who were struggling. I also worked with youth offenders and those in child protection. I realized I was increasingly drawn to working with children. Their experiences resonated with some of mine when I was younger.

I was once assigned to help an elderly woman living alone who was being subjected to abuse in her community – just like my mum during the Berkshire years. A group of youths used to steal her benefit money every Thursday then take over her home every weekend to host parties. She'd be terrified, locking herself in her bedroom and literally living off cat food until they left on a Sunday evening. It took me months to get her rehoused in a home for the elderly and I had sleepless nights worrying for her safety in the meantime. When I finally succeeded in securing a place for her, she thanked me for saving her life.

Throughout my many years of work with children, I've come to realize that some attitudes to how children should be treated haven't changed since the 1960s. I've worked with children who have been burned deliberately by having cigarette butts stubbed out on them, or who have been branded with hot irons or heaters. The worst case I witnessed was that of a child who had been held against a heater until the bars had seared into her flesh, branding her for life. I still hear phrases from adults today such as:

'Spare the rod, you spoil the child.'

'I have brought this child into the world, I can send them to the next.'

Then there were children who were beaten and who sustained fractures or broken bones. Babies left with irreversible brain damage, having been shaken violently or thrown against walls or onto the floor. Children caught in the crossfire between two warring parents and getting injured physically. Not to mention the numerous cases of beatings with belts, slippers, sticks and fists – anything to hand – planned or otherwise. There were far too many cases of children suffering trauma, not only through seeing their parents physically fighting with each other, but also those who were mentally scarred for life after seeing their mother or father murdered in front of them.

I've also had too many encounters with children and babies who have been sexually abused. Excuses given include:

I was drunk and didn't know.

He or she asked for it in the way they kissed me or cuddled me.

I'm only initiating her to lessen the trauma of having sex for the first time on her wedding night.

I didn't do it – he or she is fantasizing.

The saddest cases are those children who are left maimed for life emotionally and/or physically through such abuse. The happiest moments for me are when a child who has been rescued thanks me – not necessarily with words, but with a beaming smile. Or seeing a child who sleeps through the night without suffering from nightmares or soiling themselves. Or one who can hug their foster or adoptive parent without fear of being abused, as they've learned to trust people again.

By far the biggest number of children I encounter are those who have suffered neglect. It's these children who haven't been looked after as they should simply because a parent doesn't know how to care for them, invariably because they were neglected in their own childhoods so knew no better. Either that, or maybe the parent or parents prioritized drugs, alcohol or even the family pets over the children's needs.

I've seen children who have been starved deliberately, rooting through bins on their estate or knocking on neighbours' doors, begging for food. Children who are inadequately clothed for the weather, and no matter how much help is given, still continue to be dressed in that attire. Children who sleep on floors or on dirty mattresses. Or those who live in filthy homes that are infested with vermin or cockroaches. It may be that they've never washed and that they arrive at school in dirty, unkempt clothing with unclean, tangled, matted hair sometimes crawling with lice. Or they may have spots all over their body caused by bed bugs or mites. Some have even strongly smelled, perhaps not been taught to wash, or who have lived in such abject poverty that their parents didn't have heating to warm the water for a bath or wash.

Some have parents who are genuinely too poor, but the children I've worked with have been deliberately left in such conditions, and no matter how much help I may give a parent, they still might not change their habits. The most rewarding cases, though, are when a parent does realize the suffering their child has experienced. Those who are anxious to change and do so gratefully with a little assistance. For some, it's just a case of showing them the right way.

I've even been asked to see one parent who wished for their child to come into care. The parent pulled the scared and trembling child in front of me then started ranting.

'You f'ing need to take this f'ing bastard into your care. He keeps f'ing swearing at me!'

I asked a colleague to take the child into the kitchen for milk and biscuits so I could talk to the parent about the impact of emotional abuse. Not only that, but I also told them that children are known to mimic their parents' actions and behaviours, which is where the child was no doubt getting their behaviour from in this case. The mother was offered a social worker to help her to understand what she was doing and I left with her screaming that I'd been an 'f'ing waste of space and time', the child beaming back and waving cheerfully as we left the building. If children are continually sworn at and called all manner of names, it has a negative impact on them. When they're shouted at in public, deliberately humiliated and put down at every turn, any value and belief they may have had in themselves and their worth shrivels to nothing.

Before I start my day, it's always with a prayer and an assurance that I'll be guided in my work. I may never have chosen to become a social worker, but it turned out that I actually couldn't have picked a better job.

Every child I encounter resonates with my own childhood experiences in one way or another. Because of my background, I've been able to empathize with the hundreds of vulnerable children I've worked with – and I know that I wouldn't be the person I am today without having met those children. As my name means 'mother of India', or 'mother of many children', I've certainly lived up to being a Bharti, even though the children I've helped weren't biologically mine. My heart reaches out to adopted children and young unaccompanied asylum seekers – indeed, any children traumatized by any type of abuse. My biggest goal and purpose is to make sure every child feels loved, safe and secure in every aspect of their lives, so that they can grow in confidence and worth emotionally, physically and spiritually. I believe when a child is happy, so, too, is their soul.

Not all cases I have been assigned culminated with children being taken into care. One particular case required some real detective work to see what was going on. The parents of a baby seemed to be inventing strange explanations as to why their newborn had fractured ribs. It turned out that it was their six-year-old son who had caused the injury. He'd been playing and had jumped on the sofa then fallen hard on the baby while the mum was in the kitchen.

I worked hard to get them to trust me. I explained that I could see they were loving parents, but that I still needed to understand why they were avoiding telling me the truth. It had been a genuine accident, but the parents wouldn't tell me what the circumstances were at first because they were scared that the baby would be removed from their care. When they finally explained, the baby was returned to their care. I was so happy that the family was reunited.

I continue to work in child protection to this day and hope that I, along with all those in social work, continue to make a difference. Who would have thought that an abandoned child from Uganda would end up in this line of work....

~

CHAPTER 15

Full Circle

When I reached my mid-30s, I realized that my desire to be a mother was far greater than my need for a relationship. I wanted to be a mother more than I wanted a husband or partner to share my life with. Also, I didn't want the rest of my life to be defined by my past. I'd defied the so called Destiny I'd been born into – to die as an abandoned baby, to die from my illnesses, to be shot or kidnapped by soldiers – but now I wanted to shape my own future. I needed to be a mother without a man in my life.

Over the course of the next few years, I resolved to adopt a child, but I had no idea if I'd be accepted as a possible candidate. I was a single woman of mixed heritage. I also had two lifelong health conditions, so my chances of success were slim, but I hoped that wouldn't count against me. I believed I had so much to give a child.

I was ecstatic when a friend, who was a service manager at a local authority in London, contacted me to say they had a suitable four-year-old boy.

'We've got a little boy here and I think he looks like you! Would you like to be considered to adopt him?'

My dream had been to have a girl, but my heart went out to the little boy and I had no hesitation in saying yes. I went through the adoption assessment, but my joy was short-lived. For various reasons, it didn't work out. The social worker informed me that they didn't have any other children in mind for me. They gave me the option of waiting to adopt through them if a suitable child came along in future, or I could apply to other local authorities, given that I was already approved to adopt and was just waiting for a child.

Within two or three months, my friend Maryam called me out of the blue. Maryam worked as a social worker in a completely different borough. She explained that she'd just placed another child with foster carers and she'd seen a baby there.

'As soon as I walked in and I saw the baby, a voice told me, "That's Bharti's baby."'

Maryam was adamant that this five-month-old baby girl was going to be mine. She gave me the name and number of the adoption social worker concerned and I left a voice message for her, stating that I was an approved adopter and that I'd like to be considered for a baby in her authority's care. I mentioned that I felt our circumstances sounded very similar, from what I'd been told, and that I believed I could empathize with this child as a result. She rang me back immediately and so the process began.

The authorities came to visit me, but concerns were raised about both my age – I was 45 then – and my single status. They didn't think it fair to deprive the baby of the chance to be brought up by two parents. Ideally, I'd have been younger, married and without an incurable illness. Later, I was told that they were going to explore other options.

They went on to approach three couples and I was devastated. I felt sure one of those families would be an ideal fit and I became convinced that they'd choose one of them instead. I completely lost hope. Strangely, one of the social workers concerned kept reassuring me. She may well have been an earth angel just telling me what I needed to hear, but I didn't believe her, because there were other social workers involved who could dictate where my baby girl would go, not just her.

I confided in Mohinder Kaur Bhabiji, a cousin's wife, telling her tearfully how the adoption wasn't going to go ahead.

'Why would you say that?'

'Well, they're looking at three other families.'

Bhabiji was very religious, with strong Sikh beliefs. She said she'd pray for me and ask God for His guidance. The following day, she telephoned me explaining that she had a message from God. She said both He and her heart agreed that the baby was mine and that I was to stop worrying about it. She told me to trust what she was saying. As far as she was concerned, that baby was mine.

She had so much faith and I knew her predictions always came true. Amazingly, her spiritual connections were so strong that she could also predict for herself, showing that anything is possible if you're really tuned to receiving Divine messages. She'd predicted that she'd give birth to a second son but that she'd shed many tears because he'd have a health problem. It turned out exactly as predicted, for her second child was a boy, born with one kidney, which was discovered after his birth. Thankfully, he grew up to be a fine, healthy young man.

Bhabiji rang me again the next day, having received yet another message along the same lines. 'That baby is yours,' she said. 'You're not to worry about it. Stop stressing, because she's coming to you. It doesn't matter what anyone says, this baby is yours – I just feel it. I know it. I've seen it. And this baby will bring great joy into your life.'

A couple of weeks or so later, I got a call from the social worker saying, 'We've seen a few other families and actually, out of all of them, you were the most outstanding. You have that empathy we're looking for, because your background is so similar.'

To my utter astonishment, I was told I could have my much-longed-for baby. The joy of saying 'I'm going to be a parent – I'm going to have a baby!' was indescribable.

Bhabiji called me again when she heard the news. She said, 'Didn't I tell you that I had a message saying that she was yours? I knew she was going to come to you!'

I asked God for two things. One was to see my daughter grow up and reach adulthood. I didn't want her to be orphaned and I wanted to see her making a life for herself before I died. That way, I'd be able to go in peace, knowing she was self-sufficient. Not wanting to affect my lupus, the second thing was for Him to make sure she slept through the night, so I wasn't so tired in the mornings. Lupus means I have days when I'm steady and other days when I'm really tired. My prayers were answered – I got a baby who went to sleep at 8 p.m. and didn't wake until 7:30 a.m. And she rarely deviated from that pattern.

I felt such love when I first set eyes on the beautiful soul I was to take into my home and my heart. When I brought her home and then subsequently adopted her, she instantly became mine – not my 'adopted daughter', simply my 'daughter'. I knew, too, that I was following the path my mother and father had walked all those years ago when they'd adopted me. Mum knew at a soul level that she was my mother. Biology didn't matter – I was as much her daughter as my two non-adopted sisters. And my daughter seemed to know I was her mother, too, even before I took her home. One day, my daughter's foster carer said to me, 'Bharti, wherever you go in the room, her eyes follow you everywhere. It's almost like she knows you're her mum.'

We went through a process of introduction, where I'd go to the foster carers' home around the time my daughter-to-be woke in the morning, to change, feed, cuddle and play with her so she could get to know me. The next step involved me taking her to my house for the day. I remember the foster carer saying that I wasn't to worry if she was unsettled and didn't have her nap in the afternoon, because it was a new environment for her. But this smiley baby settled instantly. I fed her then changed her and she looked sleepy, so I put her down for her nap. When her foster parents came round at teatime to pick her up, they were inevitably anxious, asking, 'How did it go? Were there any problems?'

I beamed back. 'She's been absolutely fine.'

They were surprised that she'd fallen into her routine with me immediately.

A few days later, Anju and I went to pick up my baby girl to bring her home permanently. I was so excited. The social workers had said that she should come home to a quiet house so she didn't get overwhelmed. Being an Indian family, there was no way that was going to happen, so when I walked through my front door with my baby in my arms, the whole family was waiting, eager to meet my daughter for the first time. My brother was there with his camcorder to film the whole thing. I also noticed that one of the women had poured a little oil by my front door for luck (a ritual often enacted for a bride and groom when they come home after their wedding). The social worker would have been horrified at this family celebration, but we thought bonding with the family was more important. My daughter was happy and content the whole time, getting cuddles and kisses from everyone. I'd booked five months' adoption leave off work so I could spend every minute with her, and I planned to enjoy every moment.

My calling was to be a mother and a daughter, not a wife. When I meet people and they find out I'm single, some of them sigh and say how sad that is. But actually, I'm really happy – ecstatically so. My worth always rises to meet comments like these.

People decided it was such a shame, such a pity that I wasn't with anyone. They said I should have got married and didn't I want my daughter to have a father. For whatever reason, it seems people can't see beyond that ideal of the married heterosexual couple. I chose to become a single parent and that's beyond the norms of Indian society, but that was my choice and it's brought me incredible happiness. I love my daughter and that's where my happiness lies.

Becoming a mother made me look at the mothering I'd had – and I reflected on Mum's immense sense of compassion and her capacity for forgiveness. She had a true generosity of spirit that was both personal and cultural. One aspect of Indian culture I love and that Mum taught me is that of hospitality. I wanted to have a family home that was as welcoming as my mother's house, so my daughter would learn how to show appreciation for others and about the blessings of having the support of family and friends.

Mum had a strict protocol for receiving unexpected visitors. When I was a child, we'd sometimes get to go on special days out because Shankerdas had learned to drive. With a picnic already packed, we'd clamber into his car with great excitement. But sometimes, just as we were setting off, Mum would spot a familiar car turning into our street.

'Turn around,' she'd hiss. 'We're going back. Don't say anything. Let me do the talking.'

She'd get out of the car and greet the friends or relatives who'd turned up out of the blue. And when they showed surprise that we were just off out, Mum would reply, 'Not at all. We've been out already and were just coming back. I'm so, so happy to see you.' Then while we seethed but smiled dutifully, she'd set about cooking and making cups of tea. Mum loved entertaining. No way would she have turned them away – family was important.

If someone turned up when we were eating they, too, had to be fed. (I was so used to this that I was shocked when I arrived at an

English friend's home one day in the middle of their meal and they carried on eating their tea while I waited for my friend to finish.) If we sat down to eat at the table and guests arrived before Mum had brought our food to the table, she'd pretend that we'd just finished eating and say that they were welcome to the leftovers. Each guest was welcomed into our home with such warmth. We children would retreat, watching with longing as our meal was devoured. But then we'd smile – we knew the routine. For instead it meant we could have biscuits – a real treat!

If there was any food left after the guests had gone, Mina and Shiv, the youngest, got it. If there was more to spare, it was shared among all of us. We'd grumble afterwards, of course, but Mum wouldn't have had it any other way. Because we were older and more mature, the rest of us were expected to understand and accept the situation. If we'd skipped lunch or dinner because people had turned up, we'd ask Mum to make the same meal for us the next day, so we'd feel we hadn't missed out. We loved Mum's cooking. Our favourite was her famous parathas – a flatbread native to India – with a spicy potato filling inside called *aloo*.

We were brought up to have proper table manners, too, with strict instructions never to reject food at relatives' houses – no matter what happened. Donna, my best friend at school, once told me, 'If you ever visit and my mum offers you food, never turn it down. It's considered very offensive to refuse.' As this was part of my culture, too, I could easily relate.

I was a teenager the first time I visited Donna's house and her mum offered me a delicious plate of rice and dhal. With it came a bottle of red sauce. It looked like tomato sauce to me – I'd just discovered ketchup in England and loved pouring it liberally on my food, and this day was no exception as I poured on copious amounts. Donna's mum tried to stop me, warning me not to overdo it.

'But I love it!' I chirped as I tucked in.

It turned out to be a hot pepper sauce. After that first mouthful, I thought I was swallowing fire. I glanced up at the two of them, who were looking at me expectantly. I remembered Donna's words not to reject the food for risk of offending her mum.

'Mmm – it's lovely,' I said, trying to ignore the steam in my ears and the small blisters that seemed to be forming on my tongue.

She offered me a glass of water, but I said that I'd wait until I'd finished eating. As children, we'd been schooled to eat spicy food without reaching for water during a meal, having been taught that water simply made the mouth burn more after the initial cooling sensation. I'd never been more glad of that lesson that day and ate really fast. Donna's mum mistakenly believed I was hungry and brought me more when I'd finished. This time I drank the water but didn't add sauce. Lesson learned!

As I got older, I adopted Mum's warm welcomes, and so have my siblings. I've realized the joy of appreciating friends and relatives who just turn up, and I've learned to show them respect and worth through hospitality, just like Mum. Offering them whatever I have in the house demonstrates abundance – I believe I have plenty to give and there will always be more when it comes to food in my house. Trips out can always happen another time, but friendships and relationships are worth so much more. My mother taught me this lesson time and again. She lived on so little money, but somehow we had enough food to share with anyone who took the trouble to drop in. I want my daughter to know the joy of hospitality, too – to love sharing food and giving time to others.

Looking back, I now know I was placing my trust in the universe to deliver. Only then, I wasn't aware of it. Rather than resist the alternative paths I was shown, I went with the opportunities that seemed to come naturally. If I hadn't become a social worker, it was unlikely that I'd have been given the opportunity to adopt my daughter, as I'd never have met Maryam. Of course, hindsight often shows us the map of our past travels, the people we have met and the reasons for directions we took. When we're on our journeys, both physically and spiritually, we often can't see what's there. What we do have, however, is our own knowing – our instinct, if you like – and a guidance that's heaven-sent.

The adoption brought me full circle, and helped me to see the worth and purpose of my life. I thank my God for this – as well as those who the angels designated to give me the messages of encouragement I needed. Everyone I met and everything in my life had some purpose, and it led me to the ultimate gift: the ability to be able to adopt a child and become a mother – and, as a social worker, to help other children. I believe that none of these were chance encounters or experiences. I'm sure I'll continue meeting people and having experiences in my future that will eventually reveal their purpose to me or contribute to my growth spiritually.

Just before finishing writing this final chapter of this book, I rediscovered my adoption documents – the secret folder I'd found in my father's desk all those years ago in Uganda. At the time, I'd skimmed over those papers, rushing to read them quickly so

I wouldn't be discovered in my father's office. I remember feeling shocked at coming across my adoption certificate and what that meant for me – I was just seven years old. I hadn't taken it all in at the time, given that my covert operation might get me into serious trouble with Dad if he found out about it.

When Dad passed away, my documents remained in my mother's possession. It wasn't until she died that I came across the folder again, in among her possessions. At the time, I tucked it away at the back of a filing cabinet and didn't read it – I was in such deep grief at her passing that the folder was the last thing on my mind. I'd been Mum's carer for the last few years of her life and we'd been incredibly close. As with many things, Mum knew what the future held for her, just as she'd known she had to adopt me, and the circumstances surrounding her death were no exception.

In 1999, we were planning a family trip to India, but a month before our departure date, Mum started showing me all of her papers and telling me about her will.

'Don't be silly, Mum,' I protested, 'we'll be back!'

'If you say so,' she muttered, not looking up at me, continuing to shuffle through her paperwork.

Then she started ringing everyone in her address book, something she'd never done before. Every call began the same way.

'I'm going to India. I just thought I'd catch up with you in case I don't come back. It's important for me to talk with you.'

I told Mum she was being paranoid and that nothing was going to happen to her. And of course, we knew Mum could be famously dramatic at times.

Sadly, her prediction came true. Mum passed away soon after we arrived in her village, Jahan Khelan, in Hoshiarpur, Punjab, India. She died in the arms of her favourite brother, who she'd been yearning to see. I'd been helping to unload the taxi we'd taken from Delhi to Punjab, when my cousins ran out to tell me Mum had been taken ill, so we got her back into the taxi and sped to hospital. She died shortly afterwards.

Our whole family came over for the funeral, including Mina, who was now living in America, as well as the rest of our relatives from England. Some told me that Mum had said the next time they saw her, she'd promised that they'd see all of her children and grandchildren together. She'd been adamant that it *would* happen, and her prediction came true.

Apart from the memorial service we held a year later, most of us never returned to India. Mum never felt truly settled in England and it was as if she waited until she returned to India to die. She'd been through the India–Pakistan partition (when the British divided India into two states, Pakistan and India, in 1947) and had been uprooted from her home when Mum's family decided to move to the Indian state, and had witnessed many atrocities from soldiers on both sides of the conflict on her way to Hoshiarpur, where her family had settled. After her marriage came a further upheaval, when she'd left everything she held dear to join my father in Uganda – a land where she couldn't understand the language but ended up being fluent in Swahili and Gujarati, her mother tongue being Punjabi. Then when we had to leave Uganda, she suffered yet another traumatic upheaval.

When we became aware of racism and the National Front, the racist attacks on the house deepened her restlessness and anxiety. She'd often ask us to open savings accounts in India in case we had to leave again. Every general election, she'd ask if that party who didn't want us here had won, referring to the National Front. She used to say, 'Look at where we've come from and now we've been reduced to this. We must be prepared to leave at a moment's notice.' She always seemed anxious we'd be asked to leave England, too, especially if the National Front came into power.

Friends and family tried to offer comfort, assuring Mum that there wouldn't be a coup here in the UK. They provided great support, but Mum remained unconvinced that we were here to stay permanently. She wanted to die in India, as that's the place where she was the happiest, with her brothers and family. That wish came true.

Mum's death affected me deeply. I'd spent the last two to three years of her life looking after her after her health deteriorated. When I returned from India, I wondered how I'd cope with the loneliness, living in our house on my own. One night not long after she'd passed, I lay in bed weeping, telling her I couldn't cope without her. Then I heard her voice. It was really clear and firm: 'Why are you crying? I'm right here beside you. I haven't gone anywhere.'

I'd had the same message the day she passed, when I lay in bed in India, inconsolable. Mum's voice sounded so clear and pure in the dead of night then, too. I was so startled that my tears stopped immediately, and I got up to look at the parapet on the roof, as the voice had come from there. I looked for her in the light of the moon but couldn't see anything. Despite my grief, I felt comforted. She was right there. I knew it.

She gave me the gift of her blessing for me to adopt a child, a conversation we'd had before her health deteriorated. 'I can't wait to see your child!' she'd said, but when she became ill, I didn't feel it was the right time to bring a child into our family. That blessing was so important to me. When I was a teenager, Mum had told me how both her parents and Dad's had given them their blessing to adopt me. At that time, I really needed to know that I was wanted.

For years since Mum's death, I'd felt no need to take out my adoption folder. I had enough to deal with – the grief of losing her weighed heavily upon me. It took me several years to process that loss and feel ready to go through my adoption process all those years ago, and so the folder stayed at the back of the filing cabinet. But when I moved to a new house, it disappeared.

When I began writing this book, I knew I had to find it, to look again at the fading type on those official documents – the only evidence that told me where I'd come from. I searched the house from top to bottom, week after week. Finally, my daughter suggested that it might be in her memory box, where she keeps the story of her life prior to her adoption. So we started going through her papers and her photographs in a big file containing her whole life. As we were reminiscing, she reached down into the bottom of the box and pulled out a thin, ageing folder. Flicking open the cover, there were my documents – the adoption papers and police report that I hadn't seen in years.

My daughter and I read our respective life stories side by side. I felt so touched that the evidence of our two lives was found together – two souls whom the angels had connected in both love and worth.

Affirmations for Worth

When I allow my self-worth to rise,
negative thoughts and feelings evaporate.
I believe in the power of my worth.

~

I believe I am worth it every moment,
every second, all day and all night.

~

When I show compassion to others, both
my worth and my confidence grow.

~

Today is the day I say 'enough' to a lack
of self-belief, so the roots of my worth
can take hold and finally grow.

~

Despite my doubts and worries, my worth remains
steadfast and will always be my strength.

~

My worth has more value than anything
money can buy, as it helps me to stay
strong to my values and beliefs.

~

My worth is timeless, as it is part of my soul.

~

No person has the right to take my spirit
just because they don't like something about
me — my beliefs, values or lifestyle.

~

Worth is standing up and claiming my right to be free
of any emotion that stops me from progressing in life.

~

Worth is knowing what I want and
going for it without fear.

~

EVERY TIME I RAISE MY VOICE AGAINST AN
INJUSTICE METED OUT TO ME OR SOMEONE
ELSE, I WATER THE SEEDS OF MY WORTH.

~

WORTH IS HOLDING A MIRROR TO MYSELF,
NOT COMPARING MYSELF TO OTHERS.

~

WORTH IS ACCEPTING AND CELEBRATING WHO I AM.

~

MY WORTH SAYS THAT EVERY NEGATIVE EXPERIENCE
IS A FLAME. WHEN I REFUSE TO GIVE IT AIR, IT IS
EXTINGUISHED AND HAS NO POWER OVER ME.

~

I APPRECIATE MY LIFE MORE BECAUSE OF MY SENSE OF
WORTH AND THE PERSON IT HAS TAUGHT ME TO BE.

~

Acknowledgements

There are so many people who have played an invaluable part in fulfilling my long-term dream of publishing my memoir. If I say thanks a million times it will not be enough to convey my immense gratitude to Hay House for their Diverse Wisdom Initiative. This has opened the platform for writers from black and ethnic minority backgrounds to fulfil their dreams of writing. I have been privileged and honoured to be part of this programme and am very excited to continue and develop in confidence as an author, after this publication.

A special thank you to Kyle Gray – an established author (and a connection led by angels) with Hay House; my earth angel, who gave up his valuable time to guide and support me, Radica and Mpho in our writing journeys. (Team Kyle lives on in a special memory of the time we all spent together.) A warm and heartfelt thank you, Kyle and Michelle, for your belief and faith in *Worth* and for your investment in the memoir; and to the rest of the Hay House team, who have all played a massive part in the formulation of this book.

A heartfelt thanks to Liz Dean for her endless patience as a ghost writer, helping me to stay focussed (no mean feat), and to Claire

Dean for her remarkable and talented editing skills. Thank you Lorraine Millard for reading my script and for giving me feedback and encouragement to keep going.

On a personal note, thank you to my brothers – Shiv-dyal, Shankerdas – and sisters – Mina and Anju – who have supported me in writing this journey, helping to jog a fading memory or two. Without their support and blessings, this memoir would not have come to fruition.

Thanks to my niece, Ayesha, for introducing me to the Hay House family and for haranguing me constantly to have the self-belief and confidence to submit my initial chapter to the Diverse Wisdom Competition on the day of the deadline; literally submitted a minute before the deadline ended. (The rest is history.) Thank you also to lots of family members, but especially Menjit, Maya and friends (Marianne and Linda) who also gave me support to believe in myself when I took the first tentative steps to begin writing my memoir, approximately three years ago.

A special mention to Tosha Silver (author of *Outrageous Openness*), who helped me understand that, spiritually, a personal relationship with God/ess, the Divine, is possible for each and every one of us, cutting through the childhood years of confusion, dogma and contradictions of religious doctrines.

There is one priceless soul in my life and that is my very precious and much-loved daughter, Samaia. She is everything to me, an invaluable gift and the main source of my inspiration to write *Worth* as a legacy for her. Thank you, Samaia, for being a constant blessing and joy in my life.

Further Reading and Resources

Unsettled: Refugee Camps and the Making of Multicultural Britain, Jordanna Bailkin (Oxford University Press, 2018)

DEBRA is a UK charity that supports those with epidermolysis bullosa – for advice, events and ongoing research, please visit www.debra.org.uk

Lupus UK is a charity supporting people with systemic and discoid lupus, and assisting those in the process of being diagnosed: www.lupusuk.org.uk

~

Glossary

auntyji	aunty, used for older, unrelated women as mark of respect; never called by first name
Ayurveda	a Hindu system of medicine based on the idea of balance in bodily systems, which uses diet, herbal treatment and yogic breathing
bhajans	congregational singing and bonding
bhuaji	aunty – a term adopted for paternal sister
chunni	scarf
diya	cup shaped oil lamp used in prayer
ji	the addition of the word 'ji' after someone's name is a mark of respect for an elder, added to someone's name or title like 'aunt', 'uncle', 'mummy', 'papa', etc., so it becomes 'auntyji', 'papaji', 'mamaji' (mum's brother), etc. If you include their name, the name always comes first, e.g. Surinder Auntyji; elders are never referred to by name only
gurdwara	Sikh temple
kameeze	long tunic
langhar	a Sikh communal meal at which men and women eat together to show equality

bhabiji	sister-in-law
paaji	older brother
pandit	priest
Reiki	a form of palm healing that uses the practitioner's hands to unblock the energy within the body
salwar	traditional Punjabi trousers
shabad	Sikh hymn
swami	Hindu priest

~

About the Author

Bharti Dhir is a writer and a qualified social worker specializing in child protection.

She was born in Uganda and adopted by an Asian family at a time when adoption was taboo; the family later fled the country after the expulsion of Asians in 1972. Bharti now lives in Reading, UK, with her adopted daughter.

HAY HOUSE

Look within

Join the conversation about latest products,
events, exclusive offers and more.

 Hay House

 @HayHouseUK

 @hayhouseuk

♥ healyourlife.com

We'd love to hear from you!